PRAISE FOR *STORIES FROM WEBB*

"So often we read about what 'could' be done in a classroom or 'should' be done for kids by those who have never been inside the trenches. *Stories from Webb* turns that trend around by hearing from real teachers dealing with real kids each day. Todd and his staff do an amazing job of being honest and transparent about their successes and mistakes along the way in transforming Webb Elementary. From ways to be a voice for students to fun and practical ideas for your school, you'll find yourself nodding in agreement as you read these personal tales from people like you and me that show the dedication and love in this school."

—**Adam Dovico**, principal, author of *Inside the Trenches* and co-author of **The Limitless School**

"If we had any doubt that Todd Nesloney was the real deal after reading *Kids Deserve It!*, we can now put it to rest. In *Stories from Webb*, this amazing principal has galvanized the staff, students, parents, and entire school community around the idea that we can—and we must—do everything within our power to help every single child grow and succeed and flourish. The better news? He and the legions of caring, loving, dedicated adults show us how to do just that. Thomas Edison suggested that being a role model is THE way to influence others. After reading this, you'll be influenced in a dramatically, overwhelmingly positive way. Todd is a role model for all of us."

—**Pete Hall**, co-author of *Fostering Resilient Learners* and president of Strive Success Solutions

"Todd Nesloney is a passionate principal who shares heartfelt stories from teachers and learners. In this collection of anecdotes, you will be reminded why your role as a teacher matters. These stories highlight the real impact and life difference educators make every day."

—**Shelly Sanchez Terrell**, international speaker, author, and digital innovator

"Another wonderful book about the struggles, rewards, and heartbreaks of being an educator by White House Champion of Change Todd Nesloney. I was particularly moved by the stories of the Webb Elementary teachers who loved their students when no one else did, giving them the food, attention, and clothes when no one in their students' lives would or could. You will take a rollercoaster ride of emotions as you walk in the footsteps and share the journeys of these remarkable teachers and discover how they truly touch lives and change them for the better."

—**Jack Andraka**, inventor, scientist, and author of *Breakthrough*

"*Stories from Webb* reminded me that I'm not alone as an educator. There is a staff in Navasota, Texas, that knows all about the heartbreak, challenges, frustrations, and utter joy that comes with teaching. Hearing how they dealt with struggles and celebrated successes inspired me to be a better teacher, writer, and person. Todd Nesloney is a master at weaving all of these stories together, and it's evident he's also a master at leading a staff under the mantra that every kid in that school is valuable and that they all deserve amazing teachers."

—**Trevor Muir**, author of *The Epic Classroom*

"Webb Elementary is clearly a very special place. Todd Nesloney's collection of its teachers' most heartfelt moments is sure to inspire all who care deeply about the lives of children."

—**Sally Pla**, author of *The Someday Birds* and *Stanley Will Probably Be Fine*

"Our teachers aren't celebrated nearly enough for their hard work, and it's books like this that give them a voice and help us see just how much teachers care about their students. Todd & his team provide practical and inspirational lessons for us all throughout this book."

—**Josh Shipp**, founder of OneCaringAdult.com

"Todd Nesloney's exquisite *Stories from Webb* is a celebratory school-wide gathering of dedicated educators who bravely share their professional stories of hope, sorrow, and joy. In page after page, Todd generously swings open the doors of Webb Elementary and invites us to stand beside them as they push down walls and forge new paths, with children always in view. Through those stories from the heart, we willingly navigate the paths alongside them as we become the rich benefactors of collective wisdom fueled to mine our own stories that will illuminate new possibilities ahead."

—**Dr. Mary Howard**, literacy consultant, author of *Good to Great Teaching*

"*Stories from Webb* fills a desperate need we have in education today: to hear the voices of teachers who are in classrooms every day, pouring their hearts into creating a better world for their students. Todd Nesloney is the type of leader I aspire to be and the type that our schools need! He has empowered the staff at Webb Elementary to embody the *Kids Deserve It!* movement and has woven together a beautiful narrative of the hard work, heartbreak, and triumph that comes from keeping students at the core. The stories found on these pages are raw, honest, and uplifting. I believe that, like me, educators everywhere will both laugh and cry as they devour these stories and will walk away feeling affirmed, with a renewed sense of empathy for those around us, and with an insatiable desire to never stop raising the bar, expanding our own horizons, and creating new opportunities for kids!"

—**Dr. Steven Lamkin**, elementary principal and adjunct professor

"I love—and you, too, will love—that stories are the heart and soul of *Stories from Webb*! We learn from stories, and the stories by teachers from Webb will most certainly ignite your passion for teaching. Stories from new and experienced teachers will become your stories—their students are like your students. Todd Nesloney, principal of Webb, creates a passionate and dedicated teaching and learning community by asking his staff to share their stories about interacting with students. You'll love the responsive teaching that always puts students at the center. Stories bond us to texts, and *Stories from Webb* will resonate in your head and heart and help you reclaim, reflect on, and share with colleagues your own stories about teaching and learning with students."

—**Laura Robb**, teacher, coach, and author of *The Reading Intervention Toolkit*

"In *Stories from Webb*, Todd takes on the task of not only sharing what he believes about education but also turns the spotlight, and gives a voice to, the other educators at his school that impact children every day. Every educator deserves the opportunity to share their stories, and the stories you'll find in this book will break your heart, fuel your soul, give you hope, and make you want to get out there and do something amazing because, as Todd has always said, our #KidsDeserveIt."

—**Erik Wahl**, artist and author

"*Stories from Webb* is a collection of stories that, no matter the demographics you serve, will touch your heart and challenge you to reconnect with your why. For anyone struggling with their purpose in education, this book will help you reconnect with a calling greater than yourself. Be prepared to cry and be moved to take action in a fight that will require you to be all in for kids. I am so glad this team of educators armed themselves with vulnerability to share their experiences with the world.

"This book is proof that test preparation and boxed programs are not the driver of student achievement. The staff at Webb Elementary validate that by cultivating relationships with all stakeholders and eliminating excuses that students thrive. Filled with lessons and wisdom, *Stories from Webb* offers hope to all educators no matter their role."

—**Lynmara Colon**, principal

"*Stories from Webb* is a love story from educators who care deeply for the education, health, and well-being of each and every one of the children in their charge. It's also a candid look inside an elementary school where there are no limits placed on growth. At Webb, students, teachers, and administrators are working together, learning and growing every day."

—**Alan Boyko**, president of Scholastic Book Fairs

"If I was still the Commissioner of Education for the Great State of Texas, I would write a very nice, personal letter and invite all elected officials, especially the Governor, Lt. Gov. and every member of the Texas Legislature, along with their educational aide and staff members, to please read *Stories from Webb*. Our elected officials need to hear our stories, our truths, our successes, and our concerns."

—**Dr. Shirley J (Neely) Richardson**, former superintendent and Texas Commissioner of Education

"Todd Nesloney has orchestrated a book that incredibly demonstrates everything it takes to create a *Kids Deserve It!* Culture in any school. Some of the greatest sagas or movie and book franchises are defined by the second addition to the collection (e.g., *Empire Strikes Back, Chamber of Secrets, Toy Story 2*). *Stories from Webb* is no exception and wow, does it deliver! The true essence of the *Kids Deserve It!* community is built around a school's strong team of teachers, staff, administrators, parents, and community collectively pouring into students, relentlessly. Each and every story written has its unique place in the body of education. No person will find themselves outside the influence of its thought-provoking lessons, tear-jerking stories, and convictions presented to make everyone who reads it a better educator and person."

—**Ryan Giffen**, vice president, Premiere Speakers Bureau

"*Stories from Webb* provides a genuine and powerful perspective of the daily struggles students and teachers encounter in the educational setting, including hunger, broken relationships, insecurities, loneliness, and grief. It is evident that Todd Nesloney and the staff of Webb Elementary consistently strive to positively impact students' lives by providing support in loving, passionate, and creative ways. In this *Kids Deserve It!* collection, *Stories from Webb* models ways educators move beyond the instructional relationship, to build authenticity by serving both the emotional and educational needs of their students. This book is a direct and hopeful reflection on the encouraging mindset shift that is expanding the role of the educational system in schools throughout the country."

—**Joshua Stamper**, author of *The Passion Project* blog, speaker, administrator

"Wow! That was my first thought while reading page after page of *Stories from Webb* by Todd Nesloney. Each story left me wanting more but, more importantly, feeling proud to hear the passion in the voices of so many teachers and staff who understand what it means to always see the good in our kids and a belief that together, we can accomplish anything."

—**Jimmy Casas**, senior fellow at ICLE, speaker, author, and leadership coach

"If Todd Nesloney's and Adam Welcome *Kids Deserve It!* was an exploration of what makes up the soul of an educator, the second book in the *Kids Deserve It!* series, *Stories from Webb*, is surely a deep dive into a teacher's heart. In this follow up to the wildly popular *Kids Deserve It!*, Todd Nesloney shines the spotlight on the people who make his work, as principal of Webb Elementary, possible: teachers, fellow administrators, and other supporters of the little learners who call Webb home. What makes the stories shared in this book so powerful is their honesty and vulnerability. While many chapters feature instructional ideas for readers to implement right away, just as inspiring are those stories in which teachers admit to feeling uncertain of what to do next. Stories connect us. And readers of *Stories from Webb* will walk away from this book feeling connected to a new family of educators whose message is clear: you're not alone. Don't wait. Buy this one now."

—**Jennifer LaGarde**, school library media/digital teaching and learning specialist

"I will never forget sending my firstborn off to kindergarten for the first time. I was pregnant with my second, and my hormones were working overtime, sending me into sobs for no real reason. Watching my son wriggle into that backpack, twice the size and weight of his tiny five-year-old self—and disappear into those double doors where the fun, exciting world of learning awaited him—was excruciating. He was ready. I was not.

"The main thing I grieved was not knowing what his life was like in those new walls. Since he was born, I'd had a front row seat for every giggle, every tear, every question. Now, I wouldn't. Sure I would get stories and highlights after school, and updates from his wonderful teacher, but I wouldn't really know what the interior of his daily life actually looked like anymore.

"The first thing I loved about reading this generous, transparent book was the teacher's voice. We get to be on the inside. We get to hear, firsthand, some of the most moving, inspiring, powerful, and even painful stories right from the very heart of the teachers, counselors, and administrators, who are doing the real work of loving our children all day long. What a gift. Todd Nesloney has already learned the most foundational building block of leadership: serving. In this tender, important book, he steps out of the spotlight and wisely hands the mic to the ones who can tell the stories best. The wisdom on these pages is at the same time deeply heartening and uplifting but also practical and instructive. We need more of these stories. We need more men and women to answer the beautiful and harrowing call of a life in education. Todd and his crew are leaving indelible fingerprints on every little life they touch. Grown up lives too."

—**Nichole Nordeman**, Dove Award winning singer/songwriter and author of *Slow Down: Embracing the Everyday Moments of Motherhood*

"A must-have book for anyone trying to push fast-forward on school improvement. Todd Nesloney offers another inspirational tool to help all of us write the next chapter in education."

—**Peter H. Reynolds**, author and illustrator of *The Dot and Happy Dreamer*

"If you thought *Kids Deserve It!* was inspirational, wait until you read the stories that remind us why our kids are so important! The stories from Webb Elementary will feed your soul and help each of us understand why our students make our lives worth living each day. The messages from this book are spiritual and uplifting, and will inspire us to continue to fight for our most valuable citizens! Todd continues to impress me with his ability to elevate others, with no excuses!"

—**Salome Thomas-EL**, award-winning principal, author, and speaker

"Should you read Todd Nesloney's *Stories from Webb*? Only if you want to be inspired, or inspire someone around you, or start your day off right, or learn something from someone else's perspective. If not, then you definitely shouldn't read it. But I highly recommend it."

—**Steve Mesler**, Olympic Gold Medalist, United States Olympic Committee Board of Directors, and co-founder of Classroom Champions

Stories from Webb

This book is available at special discounts when purchased in quantity for use as premiums, promotions, fundraisers, or for educational use. For inquiries and details, contact the publisher at books@daveburgessconsulting.com.

Published by Dave Burgess Consulting, Inc.
San Diego, CA
daveburgessconsulting.com

Cover Design by Genesis Kohler
Editing and Interior Design by My Writers' Connection

Photos by Jessica Clarkson, Clarkson Photography & Design

Library of Congress Control Number: 2017961607
Paperback ISBN: 978-1-946444-56-1
Ebook ISBN: 978-1-946444-57-8

First Printing: January 2018

DEDICATION

This book is dedicated to every educator and school out there who is making a difference in children's lives: You are not alone, you are not forgotten, your story needs to be shared as well. Together we all make a difference.

To my school family at Webb Elementary: This book is because of you. This book is for you. Thank you for being brave, always.

And to my mom and grandmother: You taught me how to cook, helped me fall in love with reading, celebrated my passions and dreams, and always told me I could do anything.

CONTENTS

FOREWORD

by Kim Bearden

I stood in the intersection of the hallway, blinking back tears. As students filled the corridors, their wide-eyed shrieks of delight fed my soul. Cobalt blue paper lined the walls, covered with fish of every kind. Blue lights cast shadows across the cellophane-covered ceiling as shadows of sea turtles swam overhead. Crashing waves boomed from speakers, and a lively little boy pretended to swim as he walked through the magical tunnel. Instantly, the other children followed his lead. They giggled with excitement as they entered classrooms filled with beach towels, volleyball nets, and sand buckets. I could hear the echoes of their continued *oohs* and *ahhs* as the teachers began their integrated lessons about life in the sea.

I turned the corner and entered Chew and Swallow. Yarn spaghetti and massive meatballs hung from above, swinging to and fro. Faux food spilled down the walls and onto the floor. I entered the House of JELL-O to find children giggling as they put on their rain ponchos because today it would be *Cloudy with a Chance of Meatballs*. Another group of students meticulously conducted pickle surgery in the city hospital. I was mesmerized as the teachers masterfully incorporated food into lessons on subjects ranging from descriptive language to mathematics; the students were equally in awe.

I continued my journey to witness everything from a medieval castle to a gingerbread house to a bakery to a crime scene to a pizzeria. The special needs teacher had even converted his room into a grocery store where he taught his students about nutrition and math while simultaneously conducting a food drive. Every area of the school had been transformed for this special day, and the excitement in the air was palpable. This was Webb Elementary, a beautiful oasis of joy and learning, located in Navasota, Texas.

I am the co-founder, executive director, and language arts teacher at the Ron Clark Academy in Atlanta, Georgia. Our school is both a middle school and an educator training facility, and administrators and teachers from around the world visit to observe our classrooms and attend our workshops. Although thousands visit, Todd Nesloney stood out from the very beginning. When it comes to Todd, it is always all about the students, and his drive, perseverance, passion, and sheer grit made me an instant fan. We stayed in touch via social media (he is also one of the best at building professional collaborative networks), so I joined his lovely wife and him for dinner one night while I was in Texas giving a speech in a nearby town. I was humbled and honored to learn that Todd had asked his staff to do a study on my book, *Crash Course: The Life Lessons My Students Taught Me*, so I asked him, "What can I do for you?"

His response was immediate. "Come visit Webb Elementary and see all that my teachers are doing. I want them to know how special they are!"

He was right—they are special. Later that fall, I arrived on a Sunday afternoon, and Todd asked if I would like to swing by the school before heading to dinner. There, on a beautiful, sunny Sunday afternoon was a building full of teachers. There were teachers setting up their classrooms, designing lessons, and collaborating. There were teachers singing and laughing and helping one another. One group was even painting the floor to add to the magic. They laughed as they asked Todd for forgiveness instead of permission. He laughed and said he loved it! I did, too.

Many had even brought their spouses and own children to help out. Who does such a thing? Dedicated teachers. Webb teachers.

Yes, this fanfare was for one day, and it was magical. I was grateful and deeply touched that they had called it Crash Course Day in celebration of what they had learned from my book. But what about the other days at Webb? Every day can't be like this, right? Well, take away the props, the decorations, the sound effects, and the lighting, and what remains is magical. I saw the magic of relationships that have obviously been forged over time. I watched these teachers engage, encourage, support, celebrate, and challenge their students—students whose faces shone with excitement for learning. I learned about the challenges that this school has to continuously overcome and the day-to-day commitment that this staff has to creating a space filled with patience, joy, and love.

Todd understands the importance of giving his teachers a voice, and you will be both moved and inspired by what you read. I am thrilled that the Webb teachers have been given the chance to share their stories with you on the pages that follow, for every teacher has stories to tell. We all have challenges, frustrations, obstacles, and heartaches. We all have days where we feel overworked, overwhelmed, and underappreciated. We lie in bed and cry for those students who are struggling; we pray for answers to help us reach and teach them all. In a sense, Webb teachers are the voice of all of us, and by sharing their moments, their magic, their memories, and their motivation to keep doing what they do, they reignite that flame in all of us that reminds us all that kids do, indeed, deserve it.

WHY STORIES FROM WEBB?

The first words that come to mind when I think of what happened with *Kids Deserve It! (KDI)* are "thank you."

Adam Welcome and I poured our hearts and souls into the simple idea that we could share our stories, challenge people's thinking, and maybe, just maybe, eliminate some excuses along the way. The reality has exceeded even our grandest expectations.

What started as a simple hashtag has transformed into a movement. A belief system, even. It has united educators, parents, and students and created a place where people can go to share ideas, be uplifted, and challenged a bit along the way.

After KDI came out, we were inundated with questions about when we would write a sequel. Adam took a new position as a director of innovation in his school district while I kept chugging along at Webb Elementary School, so a sequel was not at the top of our to-do lists.

When Adam and I look at KDI today, we see an evolving ecosystem, a place where we can share ideas in different ways, from different perspectives, and across different avenues. And to be honest, we don't want to follow it up with a traditional sequel.

That's when I had the idea of *Stories from Webb*. After getting Adam's blessing, I took the leap into writing this book.

How often do you see a book in which one school shares its journey? Where one school shares its successes, failures, and lessons learned along the way.

Every idea I have ever had has come from the people with whom I choose to surround myself. While social media has opened the doors for me to meet and learn from brilliant minds around the world, so many of the stories I share with others are of what we were trying to accomplish in little ol' Navasota, Texas. I wanted to give my team—the people I work alongside every day—a voice. Their stories—our stories—are important. Far too often, the voices of those who are in the trenches every day aren't celebrated or given a platform.

So I sought to write an offshoot of *Kids Deserve It!*, a book in which I could share my ideas, thoughts, and beliefs and also give a voice to the many different people involved in making a child's education happen.

At Webb Elementary, we don't think we have it all figured out. We are still digging ourselves out of a state assessment hole. We struggle with figuring out discipline techniques that reach every child. We battle domestic violence, absentee parents, district and state mandates, and much more.

But we're trying; every day, we're pushing down walls and forging new paths.

I hope, as with *Kids Deserve It!*, that this book leaves you with new ideas you can implement immediately, a hope that sustains you, and a belief that every excuse can be eliminated.

Why? Because every kid deserves it.

CHAPTER 1

REMEMBERING MY WHY

If you were to ask someone what an educator's job is in today's world, they would say something like, "To teach our kids what they need to know so they can pass that test, go to college, or get a job." Those of us who have worked in education know our jobs entail all of that and so much more. In addition to educating children according to the required standards for their various grade levels, we act as surrogate parents to our students, buy clothes and food for them, teach them how to become good citizens, organize after school events, before school events, and attend extracurricular activities. When the final bell rings, many teachers are nowhere close to finished for the day. Their efforts often extend far beyond the classroom to make sure their students have what they need to succeed. Educators give of their own money, resources, and time far beyond what is asked of them. Why? Because being an educator is more than just accepting a position. It's a calling. It's what fuels them deep down. It's that drive to change a child's life.

A STORY FROM GLORIA WILKINSON
Second Grade Teacher

When our son entered his first year in middle school in southwest Houston, I volunteered three times a week. The school was designed with open classrooms—no doors, just partitions and chaos. There were fights daily, and the inevitable happened: the stabbing of a student. I was at home watching the news at noon on a Friday when a student was being put into an ambulance after being stabbed at my son's school. I don't recall the drive to the school. There were some parents in the school office when I arrived, and the principal was nowhere to be found, but the vice superintendent was trying to placate parents to go home. Along with the other parents, I stayed until we could get more information. After the event took place, I was asked to join a teacher-parent committee.

Information garnered from the committee for the rest of the year helped me decide to move our family, and I headed to Texas A&M to jump into teaching. When I graduated, I was not ready for heartaches in the classroom. After many years of teaching, I still wonder about my student who cried first thing one morning while telling me how his mother had tried to kill herself and him in their car the night before because they were undocumented. His younger brother was not in the car, he said, because he was born here. Child Protective Services (CPS) picked him up in the afternoon. He left his pencil box, and I put it in a cabinet. I never saw him again, but I kept it for two years.

Through the years, I've also lost sleep over the boy who

shared a disturbing secret with me one day during class. I had instructed my students to write about what they had done during the weekend, and this boy came up to me to ask if he should write about standing all weekend. I came to understand that he literally had been forced to stand all day until bedtime. He was not getting food, and his coat had a torn lining. I loaded him up with as many snacks as I could fit inside his coat, and I told him to hide the food. Soon after, his grandmother pulled him out of the district, and I never saw him again.

We all have those students who tear at our hearts, who touch us deeply, and it's important to be open to even the briefest of moments when we are fortunate enough to laugh, smile, and connect.

A STORY FROM VIVIAN STENSETH

Pre-Kindergarten Teacher

One afternoon, while I was working with my students in small groups, one of my pre-kindergarten boys brought me a plate of plastic eggs and tomatoes from the home living center. "Here's your breakfast," he said. As I pretended to eat, he hovered a bit and then asked, "Do you want something to drink?" I said, "I'd like some coffee, please." A look of worry came over his face as he reluctantly replied, "We don't have that." Then his expression brightened as he offered, "How about a beer?"

First, I laughed and told him a glass of water would be just fine. But the more I thought about it, the more I was touched by that small interaction. I thought, "Wow. This is powerful stuff!"

I'm sure this young child would have offered his dad a beer. It was certainly a sign of hospitality, and he was including me in his world. I have come to understand that you can't get closer to the heart than that. We must always remember how important we are in our students' little worlds.

One Thursday evening, about a year ago, I was reminded of what it is we really do as educators. It was our annual family holiday night at Webb, a fundraiser put on by our parent-teacher organization. Kids and families come for a night of games, photos with Santa, and a holiday movie with pizza and popcorn. It's always a great event. We had a great crowd, and the night went off without a hitch!

After making sure all the families had left, I walked to the front of the school, grabbed my things, and locked my office. I park behind the school, so after checking to make sure the front doors were locked, I began walking toward the back doors. On my way, I saw one of our fifth graders asleep on our office couch. I knew right away who it was—a little boy we saw quite often in the office. He's a young man we had invested in for several years.

As soon as I saw him there, I knew what had happened. Earlier that day, he had stopped by my office to ask if he could come to the family night even if he didn't come with family and even if he didn't have a ride home. I knew his family wouldn't be there, and I reminded him that students have to come with an adult, or they can't stay. He said okay and walked away. But he wanted so badly to be at school—instead of somewhere else—that he stayed after, attended the event, and then fell asleep in the office on the couch. And the worst part? He didn't stay to hang out with students who were his friends. He stayed to see his friends, the teachers.

I gently woke him up, grabbed his backpack, and told him he was going to get a ride home from me. This young man doesn't say a lot at school, and he struggles with using his words when he gets frustrated or overwhelmed. So as we walked to the car, we walked in silence.

I already knew where he lived because I'd made several home visits over the past few years. When we got to his apartment, I let him know we were home and that I would see him bright and early the next morning. He turned, looked right at me, and said, "Thank you for taking me home, Mr. Nesloney."

I almost lost it right there. This young man doesn't always choose to have that kind of attitude or use those kinds of words. As he got out of my car and walked towards his door, I was reminded of one simple fact—an educator's job encompasses so much more than academic preparation. And I knew, without a doubt, that this young man's polite, thoughtful response was the result of the hard work being done at Webb Elementary. He had seen that behavior modeled by teachers, administrators, and his peers in class, in the hallways and in the lunchroom.

We get the opportunity every day to touch and change lives, to invest in hearts as well as minds. We get to hold kids as they cry, sneak off to Wal-Mart to buy a new pair of shoes for a little girl with holes in hers, slip an extra $10 in a little boy's lunch account so he doesn't eat a cheese sandwich that day, go to a student's football game because he offhandedly told you no one else would be there, and so much more.

As I drove home that night, I was filled with a mix of emotions. I was heartbroken for so many of our kids who come to school just to be loved. At the same time, I was hopeful because

I knew my team was filled with people who would have done exactly what I had done—and certainly had before without a second thought.

A STORY FROM KELSEY KUEHLER

First Grade Teacher

"I learned just as much from them as they learned from me." We all go into this profession knowing this expression full well. What I didn't realize was that I could only hope that would be true. My first year was by no means a year of rainbows and roses. Like many first-year teachers, I was eager, excited, and ready to make a difference in my children's lives. Now that the year is over, I'm wondering if I did. I can't be sure, but I *am* certain of the difference they made in my life.

One kid in particular, and the time we spent together, is and will be forever embedded in my mind as one of the greatest teaching experiences I have ever had. From the moment he first said hello to me, this kid taught me more about life than I have learned in twenty-six years of existence.

There were moments he was so angry with me that he would use all of his force to yank me to the ground, calling me whatever name he thought would get a reaction. But like all storms, the calm would come, and with it a hug and smile. The calm and storm were a back-and-forth struggle. I was at my wits' end, desperate for anything that would work, that would help. I stayed up late and rose early, trying to come up with a solution. I kept going back to, "Well, if he was only on his medicine," or any other possible excuse. Finally, I realized I was approaching the problem all wrong.

Without even realizing it, I was looking for a solution that would make *my* life easier. *I* wanted a behavior plan that would work, so that *I* could teach him and the rest of the class. *I* wanted a safe environment, a peaceful environment. *I* wanted him to sit and focus and learn while getting along with others. The question I had actually failed to answer was not what would make *my* life easier, but what would make *his* life easier. What does *he* want? What does *he* need? I thought that a behavior plan through which he formulated his own goals and worked for them was the answer, and for a while it was, but it was only working at a superficial level. I needed to go deeper.

One day I invited this student to lunch. Just the two of us. I set up a "restaurant" in my room with music and a backdrop. We had lunch and ice cream and played Candyland. We refrained from talking about school. We just talked about life. I quickly realized what this young man needed was not a behavior plan. What he needed was patience and the ability to learn from his mistakes without being constantly reprimanded. He needed more love and more consistency. He wanted to belong some-where, and even more than that, he wanted people to want him there. He needed the opportunity to be seen in a new light: a little boy who loves Candyland and ice cream sandwiches and beams from ear to ear when he talks about football and mon-keys or being a goat farmer when he grows up. He needed a chance to be what he is—a kid. A right that sadly, as with many kids I have and will continue to encounter, had been stripped from him.

From that point on, I mustered every bit of patience I could, more than I knew was even possible. When I felt like giving up, I pictured that game of Candyland and the joy on his face when he drew that purple lollipop card. I remembered that and the patience came. Lunch with him became a ritual, one I was very sad to let go of as the year came to a close—a ritual that taught me more about life than I deemed imaginable.

The blowups still occurred but with less frequency and with more hesitation. They also came with a new sense of responsibility. I no longer had to tell him his actions were wrong. He knew. When this young man first came to my class and was asked why he made a certain choice, he often said he'd done it because "they made him mad." It wasn't his fault, and "they" should have left him alone. By the end of the school year, he was able to tell me when he had made the wrong choice. And the best part? He would also give me five little words that made all the difference: "I'm sorry, are you okay?"

This moment of complete vulnerability will forever be etched in my mind. While maybe I should have been angry at his actions, I could only be proud of how he reacted to them. Five little words were all it took for me to truly understand the impact we can make on these kids and the impact they can make on us. "I'm sorry, are you okay?"

When people ask why I'm in education, when they ask why I work with kids living in poverty, when they point out I could be in an easier area or ask why I stay in my school district, I look back on these moments and find my answer. I remember these children and how they need us. I remember my why.

THINGS TO CONSIDER

- What is your why?
- In what way can you share your why with others?

Tweet your answers and tell your story at #KidsDeserveIt

CHAPTER 2

THE FIRST YEAR

Oh, that first year. Whether it's my first year teaching or my first year as a principal, I remember it well.

When I started teaching, I was filled with excitement and utter fear. I remember not being able to sleep at all the night before my first day. Was there enough prepared? Was anything forgotten? Were the kids going to like me? Countless questions ran through my mind. And the funny thing is that same terror was experienced every single year I was teaching. So, first year teachers, don't worry, it never quite goes away! In that first year, there were countless lessons learned, many of which weren't expected. There were reminders time and time again that there is no such thing as a perfect teacher, and no matter how well prepared I thought I was, something unexpected was always going to arise.

Moving into administration was no different. All of the same fears remained: Were things prepared correctly? What was forgotten? Are the kids, teachers, and parents going to like me? And although I just completed my third year as a principal, those yearly doubts return every August.

A STORY FROM LAUREN MULGREW

Second Grade Teacher

Due to graduating in December and coming in mid-year, my first year teaching wasn't even a whole year! I only got six months to make a difference in my third graders' lives. The teacher before me was moving away. Needless to say, coming in mid-year wasn't anything like I had ever imagined my first teaching job would be. It was hard and, honestly, downright brutal. The kids were hurting from their previous teacher leaving. They had a hard time accepting me into their lives and trusting that I wasn't just going to leave them as well. I can remember after being there only two weeks, a couple of my students came up to me and asked, "So—when are you going to go back to where you came from?" It stopped me dead in my tracks. My heart was broken, and I finally realized people leaving them was their normal. I grabbed them both in for a hug and told them I wasn't leaving; I was here to stay with them. That was the day that I had finally seen progress and their first acceptance of me into their lives.

As the weeks went on, state test prep began and lessons got harder—which meant tensions rose and buttons were being pushed daily. The kids were being challenged and asked to do things that they honestly had no clue how to do. Their behaviors were beginning to challenge me and test me in ways that I had never dreamed of being tested before. I can't even begin to count the days that I would end up driving home crying and wondering what it would take for me to get through to my students or what it would take for them to trust me. It began to break me. There were many nights I told my husband that I didn't think I was cut out for this job here in Navasota, but nonetheless, the next morning I would still wake up and do it all again—praying it'd be a better day. I knew these kids needed me as their teacher and for some as their parental influence.

Fast forward to the end of that year, and the students could sense that the year was coming to an end, which brought on a whole new set of behaviors setting in. They were stressed and nervous for their routines to change. Some were worried because they knew that their guaranteed two meals a day from school were going to be gone, and they would have to live with just eating one meal a day. For some, it brought up the questions again of, "So—you goin' back to where you came from?" or the other popular one, "Are you just gonna leave us like the other ones do?" My heart broke into a million pieces hearing those questions. These poor babies weren't supposed to have to worry about these things—they should be able to be happy, carefree kids. This is when I knew that no matter how hard, long, and brutal those past six months had been, I knew this was where I was supposed to be. I HAD to come back next year; these kids needed to see that I really didn't leave them.

Summer flew by, and the beginning of the very next year was here before I knew it. I was so nervous since it was my very first, FIRST day of school with brand new kids that would be all mine from day one. I was moved down to second grade that year, so I was worried my previous kids would think I had in fact left them and "went back to where I came from." It was the complete opposite though! My student that gave me the most trouble ended up coming into my classroom on the first day of school and said, "You didn't leave. You actually stayed." It brought tears to my eyes, as she gave me a hug, apologized for all the trouble she had given me, and promised to be good for her new fourth grade teachers.

Those kids from my first "year" of teaching are some that I will never forget. They changed my life and helped form me into the teacher that I am today. All of the tears, stress, and hard times were so worth it. We teach because we want to change the lives of kids and make a difference to them, but we stay because of how they transform our lives each and every day.

Those first years are always special because that's when you find out what you're made of, as you're made painfully aware of your flaws and how much you've yet to learn. But you still fall in love with every one of those kiddos. Years later, you still recall their names, their faces, and the fun you had together while figuring things out. And sometimes you sit there and hope and pray that, during that first year, you didn't screw them up too badly!

Now an administrator, I love working with first-year teachers. It is such a monumental gift to be able to walk alongside them as they find their way. It's inspiring to watch as they learn to lean on others around them and discover that everyone has a bad day—or even a bad week—during the school year.

Education is difficult. No two years or weeks or days are ever alike. Children and adults come with a wide variety of emotions and ability levels, and the best educators show up every day, ready to tackle what might come.

A STORY FROM LISHA WORRALL

First Grade Teacher

When I first got the call that I was going to be a first grade teacher at Webb, I couldn't contain my excitement. I had this perfect image in my head of how my classroom was going to be set up, how everything was going to run, and how I was going to be as a teacher. I remember looking at Instagram, Facebook, and Pinterest for hours! I kept thinking to myself: *This is exactly how my classroom is going to look.*

At that point, I didn't realize it had taken all of those teachers years to get their classroom looking so cute and organized. I didn't know the time and frustration it took to just come up with a station board that works or figuring out the best way to line up. It was my first year, and I thought it was going to be perfect. Boy, was I wrong!

I remember being super nervous starting a new school and meeting new people. I had everything planned out for the first few weeks. We were going to do so many fun activities, and everything was going to run perfectly! Then my perfect-classroom bubble popped. On the first day, I had two kids under the desk crying, one kid trying to sleep, some kids trying to fight, and the rest running around the room. Right then, reality hit me, and it wasn't what I was expecting.

I spent hours beating myself up and trying to figure out what went wrong. Why wouldn't my kids listen? Why are they throwing themselves on the floor? Why is that one child always sleeping? Deep down, I knew that my first year was going to shape me into the teacher that I was going to become, and I had to decide who that was going to be.

My first year was full of crying, laughter, more crying, and lots of growth. Now having finished my second year, I don't look back and wish I could change anything. Instead, I look forward to what I can do better in the future. These first years of teaching are helping me become not only a better educator but also a better person. Every day I remind myself that this profession is truly all about growth.

THINGS TO CONSIDER

- What was the biggest lesson you learned from your first year?
- How can you help support others who are going through the ups and downs of year one?
- How are you still growing?

Tweet your answers and tell your story at #KidsDeserveIt

CHAPTER 3

DON'T LIVE ON AN ISLAND, PART 2

In *Kids Deserve It!*, Adam and I wrote a chapter titled "Don't Live on an Island." When I began writing *Stories from Webb*, I knew this topic had to be addressed again. It's impossible to overemphasize the power of getting connected, getting off your island, and sharing your brilliance with the world.

One of my fondest memories of the power of social media in my classroom is when we learned about a new app that allowed students to draw their own video game code, scan it with their device, and then literally play the game they had just coded on paper. It was a phenomenal experience.

One of the boys could not get a portal he had coded to work correctly in the game. I tried to help him, and we just couldn't figure out what we were doing wrong. He turned to me and said, "Can't we just tweet the company that made the app and see if it can help? We tweet everyone else!" And so we did, not knowing if we were actually going to hear anything back. In five minutes, we had a reply. And more than that, the company CEO and the game designer suggested we do a Skype call, and they would walk us through it.

To say this fifth grader and I geeked out would be an understatement. Within a matter of minutes, he was sitting in front of our class laptop talking to the game designer and company CEO about his portal and how he couldn't get it to work. After working through the kink, the head designer told my student he was impressed with his efforts and asked him to share his game when he was finished with the design. Mind. Blown.

After the call, that little boy's face beamed with pride, and he begged to call his mom and share what just happened. He also asked if he could go tell the principal what he just did. He was that excited.

LEARNING IS HARD

We live in a connected world. A world where so many walls have been torn down. A world where I can easily contact authors, politicians, artists, singers, and tech companies. But far too often, the single biggest barrier is us—our own fears and excuses.

We've all heard teachers who say, "Why should I learn that tech tool? The minute I finally figure it out, something new will come along to replace it!" You know what my response is? I tell them to think about that third grader they just taught to multiply. Next year, in fourth grade, that same child will have to learn long division or some other new math skill. Were they just wasting their time? Of course not!

Excuses. They're easy to find, easy to use. Sadly, I hear excuses from countless teachers as I travel and present workshops across the country. I hear them from teachers who would never allow their students to do the same.

The truth is learning is hard, it never ends, and sometimes it requires us to be uncomfortable. But what is becoming more and more clear every day is the difference in those educators who are choosing to get off their islands and learn from others and those who are choosing to remain on their isolated campuses and only connect when the district sends them to a conference. Those who are getting off their islands are making connections deep in the ocean waters that are providing them with countless more ideas, resources, experiences, and connections. Those who are choosing to stay on the island are only able to gain the perspectives of others who aren't willing to do more than wade into the waters on the beach.

We must set a better example for our kids. We now live in a world where we can learn from the best and brightest minds from all over the planet. We have opportunities to explore tools and learn lessons we only ever dreamed about, and I believe it's our responsibility to connect to that world.

A STORY FROM KEVIN BRADFORD

Special Education Teacher

In 2014, Todd encouraged our staff to connect with educators around the globe through social media, especially through Twitter. I had an account but had never really used it. I tried a few times to connect with people but not enough to see any benefit.

Todd encouraged our staff to keep at it, and because I'm the type of person who likes to do what he's told (a fact that surprises most people), I continued to make an effort to connect with people on Twitter. Our school librarian at the time, Kathy French, suggested I begin to tweet about the books I read and tag the authors when I did.

One of the books I fell in love with that year was called *Fish in a Tree*, written by Lynda Mullaly-Hunt. This book immediately became one of my all-time favorites. After reading it, I tweeted about it and tagged the author. And lo and behold, the author retweeted me! I thought that was about the coolest thing ever, and I decided then to see if Mullaly-Hunt was on Facebook. I'm definitely a much better Facebooker than Twitterer. I found her and sent her a friend request, and she accepted. Again, how cool is that? A real, live author of an award-winning book was my friend on Facebook.

Every so often, I commented on one of her posts, especially if it was about her book. I even messaged her once, and she sent me an autographed poster and some bookmarks for my students. This Facebook-Twitter-social media-connection thing that Todd kept pushing had finally begun to materialize into something a little more concrete and loads of fun.

So I kept at it. I would read a book and tweet or post about it. Many times, the authors would respond in some way, either by retweeting or liking my post. Some even made comments. However, nothing compared to what happened April 21, 2016.

It was a Thursday, and I was in my classroom with a group of students when I heard my name being yelled from the hallway. It was our librarian, Haven Wisnoski, which was weird because she was supposed to be out of town at the Texas Library Association Conference. When I heard her yell, I got up to meet her at the door, but it wasn't Haven who walked into my classroom. It was Lynda Mullaly-Hunt! I recognized her immediately, and the only thing I could say was, "Oh snot!" The author of my favorite book, the book I had just finished reading with my fifth graders that very day, was in my classroom at John C. Webb Elementary in Navasota, Texas!

As she stood there, I promptly followed up with the equally intelligent "What are you doing here?" Holding out a copy of *Fish in a Tree,* she said, "I brought you a signed book!" And that wasn't all. She spent the rest of the afternoon with my students and me, discussing her book. She allowed me to take her to most of the classrooms and introduce her to everyone. When it was time for her to leave, I asked again what made her come to my classroom, and this was her response: "Well, when I knew I was going to be in Texas for the TLA Convention, I just knew I had to come and meet Kevin Bradford."

THINGS TO CONSIDER

- How has being connected affected you?
- How can you bring others along and get them off their own island?
- In what new ways are you choosing to get off your island?

Tweet your answers and tell your story at #KidsDeserveIt

CHAPTER 4

TWO WORDS

I'm sorry. Two words. Shouldn't they be easy to say? As educators, we teach children every day how and when to apologize. As adults, we don't always practice what we preach.

Back when I was a classroom teacher, there were many times I had to apologize to my students. When I taught a lesson wrong. When I got upset and yelled. When I wasn't as prepared as I should have been. There were also times when I had to apologize to parents.

As a campus leader, apologizing is part of the job description. I don't mind apologizing. It isn't always easy, but it's necessary. What I truly dislike is apologizing a lot in a short amount of time. That's when I feel like I'm failing at one thing after another.

Some days it feels like there's nothing but apologies leaving my mouth.

And the funny thing about being a leader? Many times we have to apologize and bear the repercussions of decisions that we didn't actually make. Sometimes I apologize for screw ups I had nothing to do with because they came from my campus—where I'm in charge. In the end, that falls on me.

It's a moment of swallowing my pride. It's a moment of putting myself and my emotions on the back burner. It's also a chance to see the bigger picture and understand that a leader takes the hit for the betterment of the team. And you know what? The craziest thing happens when we apologize. I once took the fall for a decision a grade-level team had made, and at a concert event later in the week, a parent came up to me and said, "Thank you for sending out that apology letter to all the parents. You don't know how refreshing it is to know that someone in a leadership position will actually accept blame and apologize."

There are days when we need to apologize for poor decisions or last-minute judgment calls that didn't quite pan out or failing to keep the lines of communication open. And it isn't just at work. We also end up apologizing to our friends and family. We apologize for getting upset, for being too sarcastic, and for speaking before we stop and think. Apology after apology. Some days are indeed full of them.

A STORY FROM MAURA PAVLOCK

Instructional Assistant

"I'm Sorry." These can be some very difficult words to say, yet they are very important words to use, especially if you have hurt someone physically or mentally. Sometimes our actions come out wrong, and it takes someone else to point it out. I am not afraid to apologize to anyone, especially a child. But it is never easy.

Working on the bus ramp is intensely crazy. I am not assigned to the ramp but love to be there. I do it because I love to. Seeing all the children coming off the bus in the morning, laughing and talking with their friends or siblings. Getting hugs and giving hugs to these sweet kiddos!! It gets very loud and very busy in a split second. We have rules on the ramp. For the most part, it is uneventful. You get off that bus and go to the end of the line to enter the cafeteria for breakfast or go in the gym. We don't allow cutting in the line or hanging to wait for friends or siblings. When you get off the bus, you keep moving.

It has been crazy in the cafeteria, not having enough adults to monitor at times. I learned this past week that the rules are totally different in the cafeteria than out on the bus ramp. I was trying to help in the cafeteria and was seating children down. I had already talked to several older girls about not cutting in line or waiting for anyone. I noticed that they had an open seat amongst them and told them to close the gap. The girls started getting loud and saying that they were saving the seat for one of their little sisters. I told them no, that she was okay and had a buddy helping her. We got into a heated conversation. They did move and close the gap, and their little sister sat across from them at the next table. When I came back through, however, the little sister had moved to their table. I was angry that they moved after all was said and done. I walked the girls out to talk to admin.

A couple of days later, I was called in to talk with the counselor. She asked me what happened, and I shared my story. She informed me that inside the cafeteria they did let siblings sit together—not that I was wrong. She said that it wasn't what I did, it was how I did it. I went about my day thinking about that and realized that there were so many different ways I could have handled breakfast that morning.

Afternoon bus duty came, and I had to load a different bus—yep, the sisters' bus. I saw the older sister smiling, but when she looked up and saw me, her face went dark. This made me sad, and I realized what I had to do. I knew that I had to pull her aside and talk with her. I was wrong in the way I handled things that morning, and I hoped that she would listen to and accept my apology. Saying I am sorry is never easy.

Morning came and, of course, the bus that stopped right in front of me was her bus. What luck! Sure enough, when I locked eyes with the older sister, she immediately put her head down. I walked up to her and asked her if she and her younger sister would talk to me for just a minute. We walked away from the crowds of kids, and she still hung her head low. I knelt on one knee to see her face and for her to see mine. I told her that I wanted her to see my face so that I knew she was hearing me. Then I explained that I was wrong with how I responded to her and her little sister that morning and that I was truly sorry. Little sister sneezed, and I said, "Bless you," then she sneezed several more times—to the point that the three of us laughed. It isn't always easy to admit that you are wrong and to say you're sorry, but it is worth its weight in gold for that good feeling afterwards!

In those moments of weakness, it's important to remain hopeful. When we're down on ourselves and doubting, we must stop and remember that everyone makes mistakes. We must also remember that we can make the choice to be a lifelong learner, an evaluator, and someone who works hard not to make the same mistakes twice.

Good leaders want to be the best, but they also reflect strength, compassion, patience, thoughtfulness, empathy, and creativity. They sense when they have made a mistake, owning it, and apologizing. Sincerely.

It's rarely easy, and you don't always feel like it, but as an adult who is being watched by little eyes and little ears, we have to set the example. We have to do what's right, even when it's hard and even when it hurts.

I'm sorry—two words that can make all the difference.

THINGS TO CONSIDER

- Is there something you need to apologize to someone for?
- Why do you find it difficult to apologize?

Tweet your answers and tell your story at #KidsDeserveIt

CHAPTER 5

IT'S NOT THE KIDS

We've all heard it before—educators playing the blame game. That simple, seemingly reasonable remark: "If my students were better behaved, if they just tried a little harder, if their parents were more involved, then I could do my job!"

That kind of statement has always made me cringe. Why do we put everything on the shoulders of a seven-year-old or twelve-year-old or seventeen-year-old? Why do we make them responsible for our success in our own classrooms?

As an administrator, and someone who also travels and speaks around the world, I run into a lot of different people who have a lot of different experiences and beliefs. I have met adults who looked as if they had it all together but inside were falling apart at the seams.

When you work with kids, you have to reach the understanding that no matter what their age is, you're still dealing with little people who are trying to figure out how the world works.

They don't always know how to handle their emotions when they get upset. How does the kid who watches his dad hit his mom every night—because she "makes him angry"—know that it's wrong to hit his classmates?

They don't always stay awake in class. But how does the kid working two jobs after school—to make ends meet after her mom walked out on her and her six siblings—actually keep her eyes open?

They don't always sit still in class. But how does a kid whose parents have sold his much-needed medication on the street for cash keep his body under control?

They don't always say nice things to others. I have said it before, and I'll say it again, "Hurting people hurt others." I live by that mantra and try to remember that no matter who I'm dealing with—whether an adult or a child—hurtful words come from a place of pain. The answer is figuring out where that place is and how to help heal it.

Ultimately, educators have to move away from the mindset that blames students when things don't go as planned.

A STORY FROM JANE BREWER

Math Interventionist

It's not the kids. You read that, and maybe you thought, *Nope, it's the parents.* Or maybe, *No, it's the administration.* Maybe you didn't think anything at all. But stop a minute and consider something: Maybe it's you. Now you're thinking, *What? Of all the books in all the world, this is not one that should have "teacher blaming!"* But hear me out.

In more than twenty years in education, I have taught a lot of different subjects in a lot of different places. For some people, there are no destinations, only roads, and I seem to be one of those people. I have taught elementary music, elementary math, elementary self-contained, and worked as an interventionist. I have taught secondary reading, social studies, science, ESL, and been an instructional coach. I have taught in the suburbs, in the inner city, in the country, and in the Middle East. My students have been poor, rich, middle-class, Christian, Muslim, black, white, Hispanic, and Asian. They have ranged in age from four to sixteen.

And I have made a discovery. There are certain things my students do, no matter where I go or what I teach. There are ways they react to me, regardless of economic level or culture. There are challenges I consistently have in my classroom, regardless of content. That tells me they are *my* challenges because the one constant in all those experiences is me.

My classroom is noisy. I pass it off as the sound of learning—and 85 percent of the time it is—but my students talk. A silent classroom is not something I have ever achieved, and I always feel sorry for the students who need to learn in silence because I have no idea how to give it to them.

My lines are never straight. I try, folks, I really do. But I've never quite seen the point of control for the sake of control. My lines are quiet when there is a reason to be quiet—others are learning around us—and I don't let students take up an entire hallway, but a straight line has never been a point of pride or contention for me. So I rarely have one.

Students take advantage of me. I'm a real believer in second chances, people changing—especially children—and all that stuff. A lot of the time I'm right. A lot of the time I'm wrong. And someone usually says to me, "I would have never trusted Johnny." But how does Johnny get a chance to show he's changed unless someone trusts him? So I get betrayed. A lot.

But the point of this writing is not the betrayal or my failures as a teacher. The point is that this happens no matter what I am teaching, whom I am teaching, or where in the world I am teaching. I say again, "The one constant is me. I am uniquely qualified to know that whatever deficiencies there are in my teaching, they are my deficiencies. It is most definitely not the kids."

We are the one constant in our own lives. We walk in each day and decide what we're going to say, how we're going to teach, the expectations we're going to hold onto. I challenge you to look inward the next time you have one of those frustrating moments where you just want to blame your students. Take a breath. Don't be afraid to ask for help.

Let's stop blaming our children and instead look at ourselves. Let's find ways to innovate, be different, and create the school where every child can thrive.

THINGS TO CONSIDER

- Write about a time when you blamed others although the blame really fell on you.
- How do you deal with those on your campus or team who always blame the children or the parents?

Tweet your answers and tell your story at #KidsDeserveIt

CHAPTER 6

SECRET SOCIETY OF READERS AND BOOK PROM

As I've traveled and presented, the two things I am asked about most are our "Secret Society of Readers" and our annual "Book Prom."

First, let me start by giving a little background and credit where credit is due. I would love to claim both of these ideas as mine because they're brilliant, but they're not mine. They are, however, further proof of the brilliance of the educators with whom I work every day at Webb Elementary.

During my first year as a principal, we noticed a significant lack of interest in reading. I'm not just talking about kids not checking out books from the library or anything like that. I'm talking about a real lack of passion and love for reading. Our librarian at the time, Kathy French, had noticed this indifference, and being the kind of woman she is, she wasn't going to sit around and do nothing.

One of the first actions Kathy took was to "kidnap" all of the *Diary of a Wimpy Kid* books. She had seen kids checking those books out like crazy, but found out they weren't actually reading them. They were just checking them out, returning them, and grabbing another book. So she decided to kidnap the books and offer a ransom. The kids had so much fun figuring out why they were kidnapped and where they went!

Another time she organized an awesome "March Madness" book competition. I have never seen kids so excited to watch their favorite books compete to win the ultimate book of the season.

But the idea that has made the greatest impact on our school is her "Secret Society of Readers" and "Book Prom." When Kathy set out to change our students' attitudes toward reading, she decided to do something special—starting with the handful of kids who clearly already loved reading. You know who they are. They're the kids who walk around school all day long with a book in their hand. She wanted to start there. Why? Because we often spend so much time focusing on kids who are discipline concerns or academic concerns and leave out those kids who sit quietly in the room or always do what is asked of them.

So the "Secret Society of Readers" (SSR) was born. It started with Kathy creating special golden tickets that were given out to a select number of students. The ticket served as their invitation to a mysterious meeting in the library at 8:30 a.m. every Friday. The tickets also instructed the students to keep mum about the meeting, walk up to their teacher at 8:25 a.m. and utter the secret code word, leave class with their current book, and head to the library. Talk about fun! These kids were electric with excitement not only to take part but also to have the opportunity to share their book with other kids—kids like them who also devoured books.

After each meeting, the students could choose to take another golden ticket and secretly pass it out to another fellow book lover to invite them to the next SSR meeting! The meetings grew and grew, and the campus was cloaked in whispers about what was really happening. Students got more excited as they read more books, and the thrill of the SSR seeped out into the hallways as the kids talked with each other about their books. It was amazing! And we even had two staff members, Kevin Bradford and Sarah Martin, who joined in on just about every meeting as well.

At our school, we're all about holding culminating events to celebrate the completion of something. So to reward the students who were in SSR all year long, Kathy came up with the "Book Prom."

A STORY FROM SARAH MARTIN
Instructional Aide

At Webb we have an amazing reading club we call the Secret Society of Readers or SSR. SSR is for kindergartners through fifth grade students who are avid readers. Two years ago, we had about twenty members, and this past school year, we increased our membership to sixty students! Regardless of reading level, if a student truly loves to read, we give them the option to join SSR. Most students who join will improve their reading skills throughout the year, and for those who struggle with reading, this club greatly benefits them.

SSR meets once a week in our library for about thirty minutes. During those meetings, we start with our oath and share what each member is currently reading, followed by a special reading by one of our teachers on learning new and exciting things that one can only learn by reading.

At the end of the school year for our final SSR meeting, we host a "Book Prom." Each student brings their favorite book as their "date" and we have brunch, a photo booth for "prom pictures," as well as music and dancing. We also give out certificates of completion and surprise our promoting fifth graders with a special book to send them on to junior high school.

The students bring their families, some of our teachers attend along with our administration, and we have a wonderful little party to finish out the school year.

As a child and teenager, I hated reading because I never got to choose what I read. I was always told what to read. Nothing I was told to read was ever anything I was interested in or wanted to read. In SSR, there are no requirements. The students can read anything they want, and that is why they love it! Neither my youngest nor my oldest child is an avid reader. They read only what interests them and refuse anything else.

My oldest is sixteen, and SSR wasn't an option when he was in elementary school. My youngest is eight, and SSR has really opened him up to reading new and different books. Before he joined SSR, he would only read comic books. Now he will read novels or chapter books of different genres. Had SSR been there for my oldest child, he might not have struggled so badly. He might have learned to enjoy reading. SSR opens doors for students that would have remained closed to them had they not been given the invitation.

For me, SSR is a lifeline to reach struggling readers who are so embarrassed to read they don't even try. SSR has shown them it's okay to struggle, it's okay to have to try harder, and it's okay to like different types of books. Students learn that it's okay be different in what and how you read as long as you keep reading.

I have seen children come into SSR not quite sure about the whole idea and then end up sad to leave at the end of their fifth grade year. My favorite aspect of SSR is that we have kids wanting to get in! We have younger siblings drilling their older siblings for more and more information about SSR, what we do, and what it's like. They want to belong to something, and for some students, escaping into a book is how they cope with their own lives. SSR gives them an educational way to expand their minds and enrich their lives through literature. They can go anywhere, be anyone or anything, through books! If I had known then what I know now about reading and what books can do for a person, I'd have never put a book down.

I was one of those kids who needed an escape from time to time. SSR gives those kids, like I was, the chance to escape their reality for a bit and just share some time with other kids who love to read as much as they do. I love that we have SSR and can share the love of reading with future generations. For me, SSR is a small program that makes a huge difference in how we, as educators, show our students what books can and will do for them when they open them up and read. Just telling a child to read isn't going to work. You have to read with them; and in the SSR, that's exactly what they get. The teachers involved in SSR are reading and sharing what they have read right along with the students. Everyone recommends books to one another, and sometimes a particular book has a waiting list because there are so many of us who want to read it.

I keep a printed copy of the cover of the books I read so my students can see what I am reading and what I have read. When they ask how a book was, I love being able to help them get excited and eager to run down to the school library to check it out. To help a child develop a love for literature is the greatest gift we can give them. I encourage all schools to have a Secret Society of Readers. It is an amazing little club that will only reap benefits for their students.

———

When Kathy debuted the Book Prom, it was a sight to behold. The photo booth, the "red carpet" rolled out—and covered in glitter—the food, decorations, and the smiles on the kids' faces as they entered with their "dates"—it was *amazing*. The students voted on the prom king and queen—books, not students—and it came as no surprise at all when *Wonder* won that first year.

When Kathy left Webb, she left her creation in the very capable hands of Sarah Martin, Kevin Bradford, and our librarian Haven Wisnoski. Those three individuals have continued to grow and mold SSR and Book Prom into something truly magical.

Sometimes as a campus we need to create things that aren't for every child. I have never been a believer in the every-child-gets-a-trophy-for-participating approach to education. Nope. I want to celebrate children for their unique genius, talents, and gifts. The SSR and Book Prom do just that. Kathy's experiments celebrated kids who loved reading and who wanted to connect with others who loved to read. Along the way, it became something incredibly special.

We must find more ways to celebrate kids for their unique interests and accomplishments. Be on the lookout for those who are always quiet or stay out of trouble. They're often overlooked, but they need just as much attention and celebration as any other child.

THINGS TO CONSIDER

- What new experience can you create for your students to celebrate their interests and bring them together?
- Who can you invite on the adventure to help you?

Tweet your answers and tell your story at #KidsDeserveIt

CHAPTER 7

THE FOREST FOR THE TREES

You've probably heard the saying, "You can't see the forest for the trees." Sometimes we get so deep into our work as educators—the grading, lesson planning, parent meetings, assessments, data, behavior concerns—that we lose sight of what's right in front of us. All of those things are essential parts of being a good teacher or administrator, but sometimes they can become the "trees" and block our view of the forest that's out there. Sometimes we let those duties consume us, and we forget that the forest also needs our attention.

A STORY FROM ASHLEY JERSEY
Kindergarten Teacher

If there's one thing my kids have taught me, it's the importance of focusing on relationships in helping them grow and become successful. I can think of several kids who stand out in my memory, mainly because when I first started at Webb, I felt like I failed them. I didn't reach them on an emotional level because I didn't know how, I was inexperienced, and I felt inadequately supported.

Over the last few years, I've noticed that through their responses to kind words, gentle tone, and firm communication of my expectations, I started to see positive changes in the way they interacted with each other and with me. I stopped yelling, I stopped threatening them, I stopped taking things away that they enjoyed; and instead, I let them hug me, tell me they love me, and I actually said it back and meant it. I started giving them personal compliments and asking about their home life or activities outside of school. And when they did something they weren't supposed to, I conferenced with them (we had little chats) about who makes the choices and what those choices bring us. I always made sure each one (even those who I was not their biggest fan) knew they could trust me to take care of them and be there for them every morning.

I also started sharing pieces of myself with my kids, things I liked, what I did at home the night before, what I was making for dinner. I talked a lot about my cats and my chickens. Ultimately, I let them know that I, too, trusted them with who I was as their teacher, but mostly as a person just like them! This is especially important for me because I don't share much, and I'm not overly emotional to anyone except family. Sadly, those kids my first year really knew nothing about the real me.

I now see the importance of spending a little extra time allowing all of us to get to know one another. "Share Time" is what we call it. This type of interaction between the students and me has improved their behavior and my ability to get through to them, to get them to understand and grasp what I'm trying to teach and what they are trying to learn. I teach five-year-olds, and every person I tell always seems to feel bad for me, or pray for me, or bless me. Yes, it's hard, but really every day is a new adventure, and I feel blessed to be loved by my kids and learn new things from them about myself and life in general every day.

Recently, I was asking my advisor, "Am I doing okay?" and "Am I doing enough?" and "I feel like I'm getting it all wrong." I had felt like I was getting lost in the giant forest of education and couldn't see myself making any progress. It was like that image in the movies where they enter the forest and every turn feels like they're just walking in a circle and not really getting anywhere. When I spoke with my advisor about all of these concerns, she looked at me and said, "Todd, you can't see the forest for the trees." She reminded me that sometimes we need someone in our lives to grab us by the shoulders, look into our eyes, and say, "Stop. Take a step back. Look at the big picture for a moment and realize that what you're doing matters."

This moment also led me to another revelation. I have two friends I talk to on a daily basis, and these two friends are absolutely fantastic educators. One is in a newer position outside of the classroom, but still in education, and the other is dealing with that first year in the classroom. When I hear about the incredible work they're doing, I am blown away time and time again. Yet every time I tell them how awesome they are or how I'm stealing one of their ideas, they say things like, "It's really not that great," or "I could be doing better," or "I'm not as great as _____." How can these two not see how talented they are? How can they not see how they're twice the educator I was at that point in my career? I admire their work and steal their ideas on a daily basis.

But I often tend to respond the same way. I regularly feel like my stuff is junk when I see the greatness of others. I feel like a failure, like someone who really shouldn't be sharing ideas because there are voices far stronger, far more creative, than mine. And I realize all I see are the trees around me. I'm not looking at the whole forest.

That kind of thinking is counterproductive. I need to stop doubting the gifts I have been given and believe my voice holds worth. It's funny to say that when I've had some great experiences and opportunities in my life. Heck, I even co-wrote a book! But doubt and self-worth are two things I am working on daily. Some days it's easier than others.

I write this to share my struggle and to show that we all deal with insecurity. We all get lost in the trees.

A STORY FROM ANNA WILKERSON

Fourth Grade Teacher

My story is short and sweet, and it's about one of the most powerful moments I have experienced in my career. Having been a teacher only a short time, it's common for me to feel inferior. I try my heart out and pour my soul into what I do on a daily basis, but I never feel like I measure up to the standard of those around me. I think this is an all-too-frequent feeling that educators have, and one I suspect will never go away for me.

This past 2016-17 school year was my second year of teaching, and, of course, I had some challenging students, as I will every year. One particular student I'll call Johnny. Johnny had a heart of gold and was very bright, but he struggled with ADHD and often put forth little effort. I worked all year to find his interests, engage him, and even partnered him with others who would push him. By the end of the year, I felt I had done little to impact him, despite my best efforts.

I was wrong. At our end-of-year party, Johnny's mother and brother attended. As always, end-of-year parties are a whirlwind, but Johnny's mother made a point to pull me aside to tell me something that will stick with me for the rest of my career. She told me that until this year, her son didn't like school, but now he talked about it constantly and looked forward to coming every day. She thanked me.

Fighting back tears, I thanked her for the kind words and told her that it had been a joy to have her son in my life. At that moment, I realized that despite all the feelings of inferiority throughout the year, I had done something right. I had impacted at least this one child and had changed his view on education.

Today I choose to **rest in the fact that I come** to work and give everything I have, every day, for these kids. Some days are a success, and other days are not. But each day, I will go to bed knowing that I will wake up and try again tomorrow. These kids need us to own our genius, as Angela Maiers says, and to bring our best for them every day.

Don't get lost in the trees. Step back and enjoy the beauty of the forest.

THINGS TO CONSIDER

- Tell about a time you got lost in the midst of the trees.
- What daily reminders do you have in place to keep you focused on the big picture as well as the details?

Tweet your answers and tell your story at #KidsDeserveIt

CHAPTER 8

IT'S OKAY TO GRIEVE

I once saw an image of an iceberg with a caption underneath that said, "Ninety percent of what is happening goes on unseen, beneath the surface." I have found that to be true time and time again.

A STORY FROM SUE AMBRUS

Head Start Liaison

Throughout my time at John C. Webb Elementary, I have had several opportunities to grieve. I say *opportunities* that, in the long run, have been growth experiences. At the time, however, these times seemed endless.

One kind of loss was the loss of a student. The physical loss. The death of a student is something I don't think any of us will ever get used to or entirely get over. Our hearts break for the families but also for our school families. We suffer in the same way. One of our sisters or brothers is gone from us. It is a time to be sad but also a time to talk and share—a time to let our feelings be felt and to learn how to move on with our lives. Again, my Webb family has been here to help me through these times. The support and love that comes from a school family is as real and comforting as that from a biological family, sometimes even more so. Interestingly, the response is the same when there is a loss in a member of my biological family or a member of our staff. After twenty-three years, this is as much my family as the one I have at home.

The other kind of loss I want to address is the loss of self. Sometimes things happen that get you so beaten down you forget who you are and what you are here to do. It's like the light has been sucked right out of you. I had an experience like that several years ago. I was teaching first grade at the time, and I had a series of difficult classes—the kind that only I could deal with. Subs would come to my class once, then they wouldn't come back. My students were okay for me but not for anyone else. They were a handful. This was for about three or four years in a row. During that last year, I had a particularly difficult group. One child tried to throw an overhead projector at a substitute. One ran away and made it almost to the highway before someone was able to catch up with him. Another one would just trash the classroom. I would have to take the entire class out into the hall, so they would be safe when he got into one of those moods. Needless to say, it was a challenging year.

Every year we had to give "benchmark" tests. Again, to get the children ready to take the state mandated tests when they got to third grade. My class did not do very well on the first go-round that year. I remember thinking that it was going to be hard to get them caught up. I worked and worked with these students, and by the second go-round, only four students didn't pass the test. I was thrilled. Given the working conditions,

I thought they did a super job! It was shortly after that when I was called into the office. I was told that I did not seem to be a good fit in first grade and that my reading scores were not up to standard. I was given a choice of going back to kindergarten or taking the job as the liaison for Head Start. I was crushed. I did not think I would ever recover. My spirit was completely broken at that point. As life would have it, I was on my way to a church retreat weekend that day. So by the sounds of the river and relaxing with friends, I was able to make my decision. I knew it was the right decision, and I had a great peace within myself. I went back with a renewed spirit. I just decided that this was going to be the best thing that could ever happen, and I was going to make the best of it.

As is turns out, I was elected Teacher of the Year that year by my peers and started on my job as the liaison to Head Start. I tell everyone I have the best job in the world because I get to be "grandma" to sixty-eight three-year-olds every year. I get to work with them and their teachers. I get to model and mentor. When I showed up for my first day of work at Head Start, I thought I had died and gone to heaven. I'm still there. I had to mourn not having a class of my own and not being a part of the larger group, but all-in-all, I couldn't ask for more. Now I have the best of both worlds. I am able to coach UIL chess, work with the pre-K teachers when needed, and maintain my relationships on the big campus (so I don't disappear), while still being here in my happy place.

It is said there is a time to mourn and a time to celebrate. We have some of both on almost a daily basis. Loss of friends who move to new schools, loss of school families when TEA decides your school is not good enough so they split you into separate pieces, and losses when people actually die. But we learn and grow from all of these experiences. We lean on each other and we band together. It helps us to strengthen our relationships and helps us to examine our hearts. Eventually, we look back and see how far we have come and how much we have healed. Then we can help others.

One thing we have to remember is that we're all fighting a battle. Some of these battles are bloody and do quite a bit of damage to the heart. Others go unseen by the masses at large. But they're there, and sometimes they hold a grip over our hearts that feels inescapable.

A STORY FROM JESSICA MCHALE
Second Grade Teacher

September 2012 is a year I will never forget. While most teachers were settling into their teaching routines, I was wondering why I wasn't offered a teaching position for my first year. You know the saying "God works in mysterious ways"? Well it's true.

Little did I know that the Summer of 2012 would be the last summer I had to spend with my dad. My dad was murdered September 23, 2012. I was at my house when it happened. It was the next door neighbor that did it, and I still remember hearing the gunshot. Most of you right now are probably going, "No way!" or "Oh my gosh!" I have to admit it was a very hard time for my family and especially for me. I was the one who had to help mom handle the funeral stuff, I was the one who called most of the family, and I was the one who had to be the adult and put all my grief aside to do what was best for everyone else. I had to be the strong one.

It took me almost a full year to actually let the grief out, and when I did, I didn't think I could stop. I remember crying so hard that I lost my breath and was gasping for air. Why did I wait a year to grieve? I'm not sure. Maybe it was because I was too busy being strong for my mom, younger brother, niece, son, family, etc. Maybe it was because I didn't want to believe my father was gone. Maybe it was because the grief was so deep I was afraid to let it out. Or maybe it was because I was so angry at the guy who did this, I didn't allow myself to grieve. Instead, I fed on the hate and the anger.

This was definitely not the thing to do. It started affecting my relationships, my job, my family, etc. When I finally let go, it was like Niagara Falls. I have to admit, it felt good to finally let it all out and grieve for my dad. He was my hero, my mentor, and my dad.

My students know that I've lost my dad. They know he was killed. Now of course, I don't go into detail with my second graders about how my dad was killed, but they know I have suffered the deep loss of a parent. Why is this important? How many of our students have lost someone they are close to and don't know how to express their pain, anger, grief, or fear? How many of our students just need something they can relate to you about? While I know this is a hard way to relate to my students, I know by sharing this story with them about my dad, it connects me to them on a deeper level. I also know it has helped some of my students with their questions, concerns, and pain when they have lost someone close to them. Some of my students have come to me and hugged me with tears in their eyes while they told me they lost their aunt, uncle, papi, or other family member and wanted me to know. Some just want the shoulder, some want the hug, some want to talk, and some just needed someone to know their pain.

I listen to every heartbreaking story, give words of encouragement and love, and then send them to the counselor if they need it. To these kids, having someone listen to them and validate their concerns, fears, and grief is something that doesn't always happen. I may be there for them, helping them through their sorrow, but in truth, they are helping me through mine too.

I've learned it's okay to grieve and that everyone will do it at their own pace. I've learned that we don't have to be teachers of steel all the time. We can share stories with our kids and relate to them, let them see we're human too and going through this thing called life together. Sharing my story with them is sometimes hard, but I feel it's made me a better teacher because of it and has made my students realize it is okay to grieve.

———

Like everyone else, I've experienced my share of loss. One of the first funerals I can remember attending was that of a little boy named Adam. He was a four-year-old I had worked with in different capacities at church. He passed away unexpectedly while I was a senior in high school. It was the first time I truly felt like my heart had been ripped out because attending the funeral of a child is unlike anything else.

Then during my first few years of teaching, my grandmother passed away. She was my own personal cheerleader, a huge part of the man I am today. I wrote about the impact she made on my life in *Kids Deserve It!* and spoke publicly about her—for the first and only time—in my TEDx talk.

The only other major loss I can recall is a college student named Natalie. Natalie was the daughter of a co-worker of mine and the best friend of Liz (my wife). She passed away after a head-on car collision when she was barely out of high school. I remember my wife getting the phone call and us rushing to the hospital to be with the family. Natalie had been placed on life support, and her family faced the terrible predicament of deciding when to turn off those machines. Even more clearly, I remember walking into her hospital room with my wife and my two sisters-in-law and watching as they told their best friend goodbye and gave her one final hug. That raw anguish almost brought me to my knees.

A STORY FROM LAUREN MUSICK
Fourth Grade Teacher

Sometimes life is not as easy as it is supposed to be.

People think of having children and growing their families, and many times, they just assume it will happen as naturally and effortlessly as breathing or gaining your "freshman fifteen" when you go off to college. While effortlessly works for some, hard with a dash of "Are you kidding me?" is how I roll.

My husband, Stu, and I met, dated, and married in an eight-month time period. We knew within the first two weeks of dating, we were in it for life. As I was in my late twenties and he was in his later thirties, we decided to start trying to have a family a few short months after our wedding day.

There is something magical about seeing your first positive pregnancy test. From the very second you see the lines or read the words, you are a parent. You have a plan for your child, a love for your child, and you know your life will never be the same. Some people wait to share the news after the twelve-week mark passes, but I was too excited. We told everyone we saw! Our first baby was due on Thanksgiving Day, 2008.

At our first sonogram, the doctor said the baby wasn't looking like it should, and two weeks later, at ten weeks along, the miscarriage was confirmed. It was the week before Mother's Day. We named our baby "Hope" and mourned her as though we had held her in our arms.

There is something terrifying about seeing your first positive pregnancy test after a miscarriage. One month after losing Hope, we were pregnant again.

Being pregnant after a miscarriage does not erase the memory of the child you lost. It was such an interesting time emotionally, bouncing from happiness for this new life, to fear of another loss, to hope for the future, to not wanting to plan ahead "just in case," to just overwhelming sadness. Just when I thought I was healing, grief and anger would overwhelm me, and I was back to square one.

During this time, my dad told me something I would never forget and would share with many other people in their time of mourning. He said grief is like the ocean. Some waves are small, and you can easily manage through them, while other waves are so strong they knock you off your feet. Waves come in their own time, with their own tenacity, and we aren't promised that a big one won't take us down when we are not expecting it. I found such comfort in the fact that it was okay that I had no control . . . and for a control freak like me, that was a big deal! Job 1:21 was the verse that rolled through my head during this time: "And he said, 'Naked I came from my mother's womb, and naked shall I return. The Lord gave, and the Lord has taken away; blessed be the name of Lord.'" Trusting and rejoicing in God in our weakest times of devastation can be excruciating, but it is also essential. We cannot make it through a day in this life, good or bad, without Him.

Fast forward nine months, and our sweet baby Emma Jewel was born. Fast forward another seven months, and we were unexpectedly pregnant again! Since we had a previous miscarriage, our doctor scheduled a sonogram a little earlier than normal to make sure things were looking like they should.

Long story short, things were not normal. I was diagnosed with a partial molar pregnancy. When this happens, the cells that form the baby form incorrectly, and the pregnancy is not viable. There was a lot more medical jargon involved, but all I knew was, we had lost another one. We named our baby "Faith" and had little time to mourn because of the next round of madness. Apparently, one in one-thousand pregnancies is a molar pregnancy and, of those, 2 percent turn into cancer. It was my lucky day. I had won the 2 percent cancer lottery! The next several weeks to months were a blur of oncology appointments, surgery to put a port in my arm, and chemo treatments . . . all with a baby at home that I wasn't supposed to be around because my immunities were low from the chemotherapy. My husband was absolutely my rock throughout this time, and there is no way Emma and I would've made it through if it wasn't for him.

God, again, blessed us, and I only had to endure three of the six chemo treatments scheduled, and the cancer was 100 percent cured. After a year free of chemo, we were able to try one more time and our miracle baby, Brennan Hope, came to be.

To this day, almost a decade later, I still grieve the children that were taken from me. I believe their short lives had a purpose and that they are under Jesus' loving care until I can see their sweet faces in Heaven.

Grief and anger come hand in hand so many times. I believe God is big enough to hear our anger when we don't understand His plan. I distinctly remember a car ride on Highway 80 between Longview and Marshall when I screamed and cried until I finally had to pull over. I was so angry that He had allowed my hurt and wanted Him to know it. It was there that He held me. I will never know the complete purpose for our losses, but I know there was one. I also know that God knows, and that can be enough.

It has taken me years to work through many of my emotions. At the time of my four pregnancies in four years with a 50 percent success rate, I was a children's minister on staff at a church in Marshall, Texas. I never took the time off to properly process, and my grief turned into bitterness and an overall jadedness. Grief has a way of not letting go until you have dealt with it. I needed time to work through things. Now that I am in the public education system, I can see how going through the loss, pain, grief, and emotions of that transforming time in my life has made me a more aware teacher. I didn't experience the power of many of those emotions until my late twenties and early thirties. Some of my fourth graders already have. It is amazing how pain brings people together and forges commonalities across age, race, gender, religion, and so many other things that try to divide us.

I have only been at John C. Webb Elementary a short time. Looking into some of these little, wide eyes, I can only imagine some of the "life" that has been experienced in such a short amount of time. It is okay to grieve. In fact, it is necessary to grieve. Just like the picture that nature paints us year in and year out, life comes from death. Fall gives way to winter, and from that stillness, everything in spring is reborn. I believe strength comes from the healing that occurs when you allow yourself to be fully crushed but then press on to be rebuilt.

Only then are you able to hold tight to the memory of what was lost and move forward to make that loss matter.

Loss is never easy. It leaves holes that are impossible to fill. In its wake, there are days that are better than others, but the sadness remains.

I've dealt with my share of "iceberg" battles—those that only a few of my closest friends know about. One of those battles was with my grandfather, the man who was married to my grandmother. Like my grandmother, he had begun to deal with health issues. My mom always tells the story that six months before I was born, he was diagnosed with cancer and told he had less than six months to live. Thirty years later, he was still around. He was a fighter, just like my grandmother. It made sense that they were a perfect match and one of the best examples of what a marriage could and should be.

My grandmother was my grandfather's entire world. After she passed, he would go to her gravesite every single day. Rain or shine. He always said he had to share with her what happened during his day. As the years passed, my grandfather faced more cancer-related health issues and continued to deteriorate. One day my father called me to suggest that I make some time to visit my grandfather, and I realized his condition must have become quite grave. His doctors had, in fact, said he had only a week or so left to live.

On a Sunday, my wife and I drove to the hospital. I had seen my grandfather in a hospital many times as he'd been sick my whole life, but I was unprepared for what I found. The sight of him took my breath away. He was a shell of himself, tired and frail—not the man I grew up with and looked up to. Not the man who had fought so many battles for so many years.

He recognized me and my wife, Liz. He said hello and explained that he couldn't get out of bed anymore because his legs had given up. And that was it. He couldn't say anything more, and he fell asleep a few seconds later. But I wanted to be with him, so I sat there. I stayed next to him, quiet and still. At some point, I knew I had to leave before I fell apart. He was so knocked out, he couldn't be stirred, so I leaned down, touched his arm, and said goodbye.

It's so hard to explain what it feels like to look at someone you've known your entire life, someone you love so deeply, and tell them goodbye. The only other time I've had to do that is with my grandmother. It ripped my heart out then, and having to do it again with her other half brought back every memory.

As it turns out, I didn't actually fall apart until I was able to write about my grandfather. I needed to release it, I guess. I often feel like I have to be the rock for my family, that I have to stay strong and hold it together at home, at work, and every-where in between. But I've realized it's okay to break, to cry uncontrollably. It's okay to ask for help and to let our pain spill out in front of others. It's okay to grieve. I'm especially fortunate to have an incredible group of guys who check on me and know things going on in my life.

My grandparents taught me many life lessons about love, compassion, and strength. They chose to cherish all the moments of their lives. They celebrated. They cried. They did it all.

A STORY FROM COURTNEY MOORE

Fifth Grade Teacher

I've lived a pretty normal, boring life. There was nothing that really left a mark on me until March 8, 2014, when the guy I dated for five years passed away suddenly. He wasn't sick, he was completely healthy, and he was young—too young to die. It crushed me and changed me in many ways. I learned a lot about myself and forgiveness during the time after his life ended. There were days I didn't know if I could get out of bed, but I had to press on for him, his family, our friends. They depended on me to be the strong one, and it was a lot to take in. I can't tell you much about the four years that have gone by since he died because some days are good and others are still hard, but I can tell you I'm a stronger person because of this experience. It has made me the individual and even the teacher I am today. I am compassionate and forgiving because I truly understand the meaning of the words: "You never know when today will be your last."

It's interesting because my loss is very relatable with a lot of my students. So many of them are hurting and have experienced loss like mine—the kind that has changed them and made them feel things that they have never felt before. They feel like they have to be the strong ones for their families. It is a constant reminder of losing Bryan because I know how heavy that burden is to carry. It is like being in a swimming pool with weights tied around your ankles, pulling you down when you just want to get to the side. It constantly reminds me that we all have scars that will stay with us forever. For me, I have an actual scar that I got when I was with Bryan, and it is a daily reminder of how precious life really is and how short life can be.

I have grown from this experience in that I don't take a moment for granted. I appreciate the little things in life, and I've even started taking time to "smell the roses." Those practices, along with family and friends, are the important things in life. Living for today, and knowing that life is a gift, is huge. It reminds me of lyrics in a song by Frou Frou: "There's beauty in the breakdown." Sometimes in life you have to go through the ugly to get to the beautiful. Each of us has experienced or will experience something that will crush us so much that we feel we might break, but after the all-consuming night comes the beautiful sunrise and a new day to press on until we feel like ourselves again.

We know life is short, but it doesn't always become real to us until we've had that personal reminder.

A STORY FROM LAUREN NEUTZLER

Second Grade Teacher

The summer before I started my first year of teaching, I was so glowing with passion that it could light up an entire room. But exactly one week before my first day of my first year of teaching, I got a phone call from my dad. He told me that something had happened to my grandma, and I needed to get to the hospital as soon as possible. For the first four months of my first year of teaching, I spent each day visiting my grandma in ICU, then hospice, after work. Then she literally made a miraculous recovery and was doing great.

Fast forward to the beginning of my second year of teaching, and that same grandma who had made a full recovery now suffered a massive stroke and passed away three weeks into my second year of teaching. In the same three-month period, I found out I was pregnant (which was something that my husband and I had been praying for). We were so excited that we told my entire family on Christmas Eve. Then, on Christmas Day, I had a miscarriage, and three months later, I suffered a second miscarriage.

In May of this past year, we found out that my other grandma's stomach pains were stage four pancreatic cancer. Three and a half weeks later, I sat with my family, holding my grandma's hand, as she took her last breath.

I say all of this to tell you that being an educator is not for the faint of heart. It is not a profession that you can do alone. My team, co-workers, and administrators, literally and figuratively, wrapped their loving arms around me. They took care of my every need in every time of loss and grief. At first, I tried to be strong and do everything on my own. I tried to pretend like I was fine and could handle it all. I will never forget this past May, when I was sitting in my classroom crying. Two of my teammates came into my room to check on me. When I told them that I desperately wanted to leave school to go spend time with my grandma, but I had so much still to do, they looked at me and said, "Get your purse, get your keys, and go spend time with Mamaw. Make us a list and we will stay and get it done for you." And you know what? They did EVERYTHING on my list and more. They did not hesitate. They took care of me because in those times when we can barely lift our head up to face another day, we have to lean on others; and sometimes they may even have to carry us for a little while.

When I had both of my miscarriages, Todd and the rest of our admin team told me, "Take as much time as you need. We will take care of your kids, and we are praying for you. If you need anything, just ask—we are family." I felt like a bad teacher because I took time off during these hard times, but I had to learn that you are not a bad teacher because you are grieving. You are human, and you need to take the time to grieve. You have to let others lift you up when you need it most and when you get the chance, do the same for them.

These days I'm trying to love harder, forgive faster, and understand more deeply. I'm trying to allow others to see more of my "iceberg" and enjoy every single moment because I never know when it might be my last.

THINGS TO CONSIDER

- What keeps you from sharing your burdens and grief with others?

- Have you experienced the freedom of allowing others inside? What did you learn from that experience?

Tweet your answers and tell your story at #KidsDeserveIt

CHAPTER 9

SOME HAVE NO ONE ELSE

L ike many schools across this country, we have children at
Webb who have no one else. We are all they've got. We're the
ones who encourage them, discipline them, celebrate them, and
believe in them.

A STORY FROM TAMERA BOYD
Fifth Grade Teacher

As we began the school year, I believed
everything was coming together well.
But as we approached the second half
of the first nine weeks, one student
began to reveal some behavioral and
personality issues. It was a challenging situation, and it became clear to
me she had more potential than she
was fulfilling. I also realized she was
struggling with self-esteem.

I had many goals and aspirations that I wanted to guide this
child towards. First and foremost, I needed to build her self-esteem for her to internalize just how successful she could be as

a fifth grader. At first, she was reluctant to accept this type of attention, but slowly we created magic in our relationship. She understood my expectations and began to believe in herself.

It was around the middle of the year that she began to talk to me about her future at a university in Georgia. Her self-confidence and engagement in class also contributed to her success. As the year came to a close, she was exhilarated to receive the most awards in her class. She excitedly told me that she was ready to show the junior high teachers just what she had learned and how far she had come.

As a teacher for more than twenty-five years, I can honestly say that students cannot survive without teachers, and without a doubt, teachers cannot survive without students. I experienced something special with this one child that has better prepared me for the remainder of my teaching career. Thanks to this young girl, I experienced the best school year to date!

HELPING STUDENTS COPE

I have students come into my office every day for "Hats Off," which are special calls to celebrate them. One day, though, something different happened. I had called home to celebrate a third grader who struggled with school quite often. He was so excited about his "Hats Off" card. As we called his mom—and had her on speaker phone—I told her the great reasons I was calling and how proud we were of her son. I then asked her, as I do every parent, if she'd like to talk to her son to celebrate him too. Her response? "No, that's okay. I can talk to him later if I feel like it."

Her son heard the whole exchange. He lost all sense of excitement and put his head down. It broke my heart.

But it was an effective reminder. A reminder that our kids come from homes where they aren't always taught about their worth and value. Socioeconomic status doesn't always play a part. These kids come from all walks of life, from wealthy homes as well as homes devoid of virtually any material possessions.

Many of the kids we're teaching have complicated, heart-wrenching back stories. They don't always come to us having been nurtured or protected or treated with kindness and respect. They don't always know what to do with the emotions they feel in response to these situations, and they act out. So often, that's when they cross our paths.

I remember a conversation I once had with a student about her behavior. She was a tough cookie, and we had poured a lot of time and attention into her for more than a year. She had a lot of pain built up inside her, and it sometimes came out in the most unfriendly ways. After one of these episodes, I pulled her into my office and asked her what was going on. She didn't want to talk about it. She never does.

So I tried a different approach. We have three staff members who are working hard to get her in a better place. I told this girl how much her teacher loves her, how much our assistant principal loves her, and how much her teacher from last year loves her. And it was true. All three of those educators care about her so much.

Then I told her the way she treats those who care about her is hurtful. Speaking candidly, I told her that some people can only take so much of someone being hateful to them before they throw their hands up. Before they walk away, saying, "Does she hate me? I've tried everything, and I just don't know what else to do!" For the first time ever, I saw something different in her. She looked at me and said, "I don't hate them. I love them a lot too."

She sat with me in my office, and she cried. We talked about how our emotions can sometimes get the better of us. I told her it happens to all of us at one point or another, but the key is not letting those feelings control us. We talked about not allowing our hurt and anger to push others away and not lashing out at those we love. I told her it was okay to be angry, okay to struggle with friends and school, and okay to cry. But I also told her we can't keep it all bottled up. We have to verbalize our emotions and ask for help when we need it. That's how we can show those around us that we're trying to change and be better.

Did I get through to that child? Who really knows. Only time will tell. I know she'll lash out in anger again, but maybe she'll see a little more clearly that we care about her, want to help her, and desire to walk with her down this road.

A STORY FROM MALLORY LAPLANT

Former Front Office Secretary

When I took the position as school secretary, I took it knowing that I liked kids and that I needed to make money. Being a school secretary made sense. What I could not have expected is that a passion for children would grow in my heart. On the same day I accepted the job, my life began changing in the most amazing way.

I never expected to form close relationships with the students at our school. I worked in the office, and the kids I spent the most time with were the ones who were waiting to speak to an administrator. I saw the same kids week after week. After a few months, they slowly started to talk to me. A few months later, they would say hello in the hallways. As I got to know them little by little, their outbursts and misconduct perplexed me. Their behavior seemed so extreme and bizarre, and I struggled to understand how such seemingly kind kids could behave the way they did.

The same student who smiled at me and hugged me in the morning was throwing books across the room and screaming at another student by lunch time. I started to take notice of other circumstances in these children's lives. Many were impoverished, from broken and tumultuous families, homeless, and abused. As a mother of three children myself, my heart broke for them. I realized that many of them were products of their environments and had little positive support outside of school. I knew there wasn't much I could do after they left for the day, but at least while they were on campus, I could smile, hug, and encourage. I grew to love this group of kids. I hated that some would label them as "bad kids" because I saw in their hearts that they were actually good people in bad situations.

One of the many things I love about Webb is that students come to the office for positive behavior. When students go above and beyond what is expected of them, whenever they reach a new reading level, or accomplish something they have worked hard for, we get to celebrate them in the office. One particular little girl—I'll call her Sarah—came to the office to celebrate an achievement and immediately stole my heart. Sarah was one of the students in our Preschool Program for Children with Disabilities (PPCD). She was very small for her age and had visual and hearing impairment. Her teacher brought her into the office to celebrate her potty training and had given her a new outfit to celebrate. Sarah was so excited about her outfit and was beaming with pride. Her teacher introduced us, and we quickly became friends. I loved when she would come and see me in the office, and I started taking time to go and visit her class too. I learned that her family had many children, and Sarah did not have a lot of clothes that fit her, and the ones she did have were torn and dirty. One of my daughters was similar in size, so I went through everything we had and brought her clothes to keep at school so she would have something nice to wear while she was here. It was such a joy to share little victories with her and steal hugs from her at the end of the day. Sarah had missed a few days of school, so I decided to call her mom and check in on her. Mom proceeded to tell me they had moved to a town twenty minutes away and were taking Sarah out of school. She wasn't able to bring her back to say goodbye. My heart shattered into a million pieces. I broke down in tears. I was scared for her well-being, knowing her home life was unstable. I was also crushed to lose this girl I cared so much for. She made my day brighter every time I saw her. She was a tiny little girl, but loving, and had so much spirit. I pray for her every night and still think about her constantly.

Those experiences were not what I pictured when I decided to come to Navasota. I fell in love with those students who had to try a little harder than most, defy the odds, and be hugged a little tighter. In my time at Webb, I found a passion for helping children and a sense that I needed to do more. I knew that I could only do so much as a secretary, and to do more, I would need to go back to school. It was hard to make the decision to leave the school that I loved so much and to say goodbye to the parents, students, and coworkers who helped me find my path. I have seen and experienced so many things at Webb Elementary, and I plan to use it all when I have a classroom of my own.

Now I know what my life's mission is, and I owe it all to "those kids." They changed everything for me.

I am so thankful to have the job I do. Teaching is a special profession. It's not something I feel I have to do but something I get to do. And I am so incredibly thankful to work alongside people like you every day, people who pour their hearts and souls, and blood, sweat, and tears into these kids.

All of these examples are reminders to every one of us to take the time to hug our students a little harder, give a few more high fives, and celebrate every single moment because we might be the only one in their lives celebrating.

A STORY FROM LAUREN NEUTZLER

Second Grade Teacher

When I graduated from college, I was so excited and ready to start my teaching career. I applied and interviewed all over my hometown but did not get a job. I decided that I would substitute teach until I landed a job. My student teaching mentor was pregnant at the time and was thrilled when I said yes to being her long-term sub after she had her baby that year.

All of that brings me to the important stuff. Before I took over her third grade class, she and her partner teacher were telling me about their kiddos. One student they told me about struck a chord in my heart—a boy who would never really talk to them or the other students. They said he was very shy and soft-spoken. They said he was not disrespectful, just rarely talked. In that moment, I knew I had a mission.

About two weeks into my long-term sub, I had a student from another class, whom I had known prior to this job, ask me to attend his soccer game that weekend. I went to his game and on Monday when we arrived at school, he was telling everyone I had come to watch him play. This led to a lot of kids asking me to come to their games. I said, "Okay! If you would like me to come to one of your games, raise your hand, and I will call you up one at a time." At least seven hands shot up in the air, and as I was calling them up one by one, I saw a little boy's hand slowly stretch up high. I asked him, "Yessir, what's up?" I was thinking he probably needed to go to the restroom or sharpen a pencil. He looked at me and very quietly said, "I have a soccer game on Saturday. Can you come?" I could not help the emotions that followed his question. Tears instantly filled my eyes, and my heart jumped for joy. I knew that no matter what was going on in the world, I had to be at that game. I went and his mom wrote me the sweetest note at the end of the school year that, again, brought me to tears. She thanked me for coming to his games and told me I would never fully know the impact that it had on her and her son. She said my attendance at his games brought him slowly out of his shell at school to a point where more kids were including him, and he could not stop talking about the fact that his teacher came to watch him play.

After reading that card and seeing the excitement on his face, I knew that would be a major way that I could connect with my students. That summer I got a call from the principal at Webb Elementary to be a third grade teacher. The first day of school, the first time I had my very own class, one of the first things I told my kids was to bring me a schedule of their sports games and I would try my best to attend. They all had confused looks on their faces and said, "Really? You really will come?!"

Going to my students' games and events has become part of my life now. I love watching them play. It allows me, as their teacher, to see them outside of the classroom and in a different light. It allows me to better understand them, and it is one of the easiest ways I have found to connect and build relationships with my kids. It means more to the kids than you will probably ever realize. Every time I go, they always come to school the next day telling everyone they can, their face completely lit up. "Mrs. Neutzler came to my game!"

They notice the little things because to them, they are the big things. It tells them you care about them so much that you gave up your time to be there for them. I promise you will notice a change in how they respond to you. Did I also mention the phenomenal impact it has on the parents of your kiddos? Parent-teacher conferences are so smooth when they see how much you love their kid. To this day, I still go to the games of that little boy from my student teaching days, as well as the games of other former students. Even though you are trying to make their heart happy, you will find that it fills your heart with so much joy! Go to their games and events. Take your family or spouse with you. Share your life with your students and be a part of their lives outside of the classroom. You will not regret it

---

Even amid all the adversity, we must have a big enough heart to love those we come in contact with; to forgive them time and time again; to shower them with compassion, patience, and honesty. We have to show them we aren't going anywhere and we aren't going to abandon them. We have to prove to them we will show up because we might be the only one.

THINGS TO CONSIDER

- How have you been there for a child who seemed to have no one else?
- When have you had to forgive a child even though you didn't want to?

Tweet your answers and tell your story at #KidsDeserveIt

CHAPTER 10

MAKING EXCUSES

We've all been there. We've all made excuses for why we couldn't do something or how someone else was at fault. It's human nature. Sometimes we blame the students, sometimes we blame the parents, and sometimes we blame our own campus or district.

In reality, making excuses doesn't get us anywhere. I've always told my staff I don't mind hearing complaints. I just want those complaints followed up with a potential solution. Complaining just to complain is futile.

A STORY FROM LISA MARSH

Kindergarten Teacher

As teachers, we have frustrations during the school year. At times, we think it is just us and no other teacher feels this way. We also sometimes think if only we worked at that school or in that district, everything would be great. But no matter what your job is in education, there will be frustrations, either co-workers, students, or parents. During this past school year, I have had to deal with this reality in so many ways, but it's helped me grow as a teacher.

When it comes to students, it can be so frustrating to deal with certain kids. We all know these students! They are the ones who make you wonder why you are even teaching or in education. They are the students who are not acting appropriately in class. The behavior varies from student to student, but we have all seen it. As a classroom teacher, you want to help all of your students, but with those challenging students, it is especially hard. It's hard because you have to look past the inappropriate behavior and help the child to see it is wrong.

The main thing I learned from working with students who frustrate me is you have to look past the frustration and love them. And that means building relationships with those students. It is not easy when the inappropriate behavior is disrupting your classroom or when the student might be trying to run your classroom. I have learned that when a student is acting this way, it is because they don't know another way to act. Most of these students act this way because they need to know they are loved by someone and that someone cares for them. They also need to know that school and the classroom are a safe place. When the student is acting up, it is hard to remember this. You have to almost train your thought process to think this way when the bad behavior is occurring.

As a teacher, you have to figure out a way to calm yourself and them down and let them know you still love them—but not their current behavior. I had several students who would act out in not-so-appropriate ways in the classroom. At first, I would get so frustrated and hang onto that frustration for a couple of days. Then one day, I was talking to our school counselor about my frustration and how could I help these students. I knew I couldn't handle it myself and needed help in dealing with it. She told me I had to remember where these students were coming from and what their home life was like. Once I started to think about this and started to really listen to the stories these students were telling me, I realized she was right. I needed to look past the behavior and show them that I loved them unconditionally. It was not easy at first, but as time went on, the behaviors I was seeing would decrease and sometimes go away. We need to love all of our students, even those who cause us frustration.

As educators, we can also have frustrations with students' parents. So many times I hear teachers say the following:

I wish those parents could help their child at home.

I wish parents would look into the daily folder I send home.

Those parents don't spend any time with their children.

Why do parents think it is the teacher's fault all the time?

Parents always think we are the only ones who can make their kids smart.

I was one of those teachers who said those things. This past year, I realized many parents would like to help their children at home but don't have the ability to help for various reasons. Some parents didn't get enough schooling themselves to be able to guide their children. We teachers can work with the parents and provide them with resources to help their child at home. And I'm not talking about just handing them some worksheets. We need to sit down with them and show them how to help the child. Some parents, particularly those at lower socio-economic levels, are working multiple jobs or living on an assistance program. When parents are in this situation, they want to be able to spend fun time with their child. They don't want to spend it struggling through school work.

This past school year, I found out my parents liked not having homework every week. They still worked with their children, but it was on their schedule, not mine. All my students got to where they needed to be by the end of the year doing it this way. I showed the parents how to use various resources, and they felt confident they could use them at home. Teachers need to build relationships with parents, treat them with respect, and listen to what they are telling us. We cannot have our own agenda and push it on them. It will only cause us more frustration and leave parents frustrated with what we are doing to help their child.

The final area of frustration I saw this year involved co-workers. We have to treat our co-workers with respect and be professional at all times. We need to build relationships with our co-workers as well. When we don't do this, it affects everyone in the building in some way, but it hurts the students the most. Teachers might not always agree with what the administration or the district is telling us to do, but we can't let our frustration negatively impact our jobs. This is exactly what happened in my classroom this year.

I didn't always agree with some of the decisions that were being made for my students in my class. I was frustrated because my students were not getting the help they needed. I felt there were ways others could provide more assistance to my students, but I knew I had no control over the situation, which compounded my frustration. When I talked about it with several colleagues I truly admire, I realized I was making it harder on myself and, at times, for my students. I resolved to do everything I could do in my classroom to help my students, to be their advocate. When I was able to let that frustration go, I found ways around the decision to still do what was best for each of my students.

So many people look at Webb Elementary and think we have it so perfect because so many great things are coming out of our school. We are just like any other school in the world. We have many of the same frustrations that educators have to deal with. We just try to work through those frustrations as a team to make the school **better for our children and** their parents.

Reflection is an important piece of any career. Sometimes it's helpful for educators to step back and examine whether they are making excuses for their students. Or, perhaps worse, whether they are allowing them to make their own excuses. Teachers have so many opportunities to show students how to work through adversity and not be defined by their circumstances. We just have to keep our eyes open and be willing to be honest about our actions.

A STORY FROM NINA SALAZAR

Instructional Aide/Art Teacher

Her name is Jacinta, and she has a smile that could light up the darkest sky. Not only is she one of our life skills students at Webb, she's also my daughter.

Jacinta was born with DiGeorge Syndrome, which is a very rare genetic disorder causing the deletion of chromosome 22. It's a very complex condition, which you will see if you Google it. Looking at her, you would never know she even has a disability. She is a tiny girl who is so determined to live a normal life.

I think back to before she was born, and at that time in my life, I truly believe I was lost. Yes, I had other children, but there was just something about Jacinta that was different. It was so hard to watch my precious five-pound baby girl endure all of the poking and prodding and being hooked to machines. Always fighting to live just one more day. In the face of heart failure, not being able to eat by mouth, and the doctors' warnings that she might not ever walk, Jacinta has beaten the odds. We were told most kids with DiGeorge Syndrome don't live past five years old. Jacinta is now ten years old. She's truly a miracle.

Jacinta has taught me so many values and brought out this love in me I never knew I had for children. She has taught me to slow down and to enjoy all the little things in life that often go unnoticed because, well, life is just that crazy sometimes. She has shown me people and complexities don't define you. What defines you is the will you have inside you. The desire that she has to be what she feels is normal is something so special because it helps her to get through the sick days, surgeries, and through the many obstacles she faces daily because she is partially paralyzed on her right side.

I am blessed to be part of Webb Elementary. I am able to take what I have learned from Jacinta and apply it toward helping children become believers in themselves. There are many children on our campus who never hear any words of encouragement outside of school. We have students who have trouble seeing the good in themselves and always find reasons for why they can't accomplish a new task. I love to use Jacinta as an example when I tell the kids they can do anything if they put their minds to it. I tell them how we were told she would never walk. Then I tell them about the day when she was three years old, and I got a phone call from one of her teachers at Webb who shared that Jacinta had just taken her first steps. It's a valuable lesson on never giving up. I teach them that failing is okay as long as you make sure you come back to face whatever it is that's in your path and try again.

I firmly believe that it doesn't matter how many people believe in you if you don't believe in yourself. I tell this to my own kids. It's all in self-confidence, which is something I, even as an adult, struggle with on a daily basis. But then I look at my Jacinta, and I see her pushing through.

Every day is a struggle, but we move forward. I tell my kids, "God didn't wake us up today for nothing!" I feel like we can all make a difference if we just try harder. Jacinta gives me a purpose, and I feel the need to share it with everyone I come into contact with. She makes everything more meaningful. Now that I have been working at Webb for five years, I have been able to witness many milestones along the way with Jacinta, and for that I will forever be grateful.

We are all given a chance to make a difference at some point in our lives. It's up to you whether you will choose to waste it. But why not take it? You never know what impact you might have on someone!

Today let's face our trials, mistakes, and struggles head on and make the best of the situation we've been given. Let's throw out all the tired, old excuses and make a positive difference in the lives of others.

THINGS TO CONSIDER

- What excuses have you made, or are continuing to make, that are keeping you from being your best?

- How can we help others not sit back and make excuses?

Tweet your answers and tell your story at #KidsDeserveIt

CHAPTER 11

WHEN THERE'S NO CLOSURE

Sometimes things just end. We don't see it coming. It wasn't expected, but it's over in the blink of an eye, and we're left picking up the pieces and figuring out what to do next.

A STORY FROM BRENDA PARKER

Pre-Kindergarten Teacher

He was a curious little boy with a broad smile and the same birthday as my granddaughter. He came in the middle of the year as a foster child. The family he was living with had no blood relation to him, but they were going to try to adopt him.

He tried so hard to catch up to the rest of the children that he ended up flying past them academically. He always did everything I asked him and was a very good friend to his classmates. But there was a lot going on in his life outside of school. He had been shuffled from place to place his entire life, and his birth mother was in and out of his life.

During the summertime, I just couldn't get him off my mind, so I called his foster mother. She told me he had been taken from them and put with a family member in another town. I was heartbroken. I wish I could have taken that little boy home with me. I know I could have given him the life he deserved.

As it turns out, it didn't work out with the relative, so the birth mother finally gave up her rights, and he is finally being adopted by another family. I hope he ends up with some stability. He was such a special little boy that not getting that closure has always been tough. Maybe I will see him again someday. I sure hope so.

___

My edu-brother and mentor, Ben Gilpin, always tells me, "Share your story and share it honestly."

So here goes.

I had just completed my second year as a principal. It was amazing—by far, the best year of my career. There were so many great memories, tears, laughter, and more. That year we truly became a family. We experienced death, celebrated new life, danced, played, and worked our tails off to give our students the best education and school year ever!

Then something happened.

The last two days of the school year were upon us, and we had many things planned. Both days were scheduled to be half-days with a noon release.

Thursday went off without a hitch, and we had plans for award ceremonies and end-of-year parties on Friday. Although the kids had left at noon, the staff stayed on campus to complete the work day. At about 2:45 p.m., we got alerts on our phones.

Tornado warning. Flood warning. Severe thunderstorm. The whole nine yards. We don't get too many tornadoes in our area, and flooding is also pretty rare, so the entire staff quickly took shelter in the middle of the school.

We were thankful the students weren't there, as this would have been our normal dismissal time, but we all were worried about them along with our own families. We stayed in position for about thirty minutes, and the warning was lifted. But soon we began to hear reports about tornadoes touching down fifteen miles north of us, then one mile south of us. We heard about buildings being ripped apart and semi-trucks flipped over on the highway. The storm didn't let up.

At about 4:30 p.m., the storm let up a little, and some of us ventured out. Most roads were closed due to tornado damage or extreme flooding. In fact, we later learned that Brenham, where I live, got about thirteen inches of rain in less than two hours.

I decided to head home—thirty miles away from Navasota—but only made it one mile through town because most of the roads were under water. Just trying to turn around and get back to school was a challenge, and my SUV almost stalled out. When I got back to school, there were still twenty to thirty employees there, waiting it out, and several people ended up staying the night. About two hours later, after the rain had slowed considerably, I started driving toward my house. Because of downed trees and flooded bridges, it took me five and a half hours to get home that night. It was terrifying.

Then, that evening, we got the news that school was canceled on Friday and wouldn't be rescheduled, as it was the end of the school year. No goodbyes, no parties, no awards, no staff pot-luck, nothing.

How could this be? We'd had the most wonderful year and now it was over? Just like that?

Before long, a flood of phone calls from teachers in tears started coming in. I wasn't surprised. Our student population is one we give our all for. We become their school parents, and they become our children. It was heartbreaking to know we wouldn't get closure.

It had to be done, of course. The storm damage ended up being too severe to ignore. Many of my team and the families we served were still without power, and some were still unable to reach their homes.

So how do you end a school year when the end never really comes? My heart was torn. Even sharing this story here brings up all the heartache of those first moments. Everything felt so unfinished.

But sometimes, when you least expect it, something good can still be made out of something terrible. Within hours of realizing we wouldn't have our last day of school, every team got together and planned a time during that next week when they would invite students to the school to tell their teachers goodbye and celebrate the end of the year.

That's family, and that's my team at Webb, who continue to blow my mind. Without one complaint, they chose to give up their first week of summer break because they couldn't go through the entire summer without getting their goodbyes.

A STORY FROM KHELI LABLUE

First Grade Teacher

As an elementary school educator, the month of May signifies so many "lasts." The *last* mornings of getting up early for a while, the *last* lesson planning, the *last* evaluations, and the list continues. However, until May of 2016, I had not realized the special significance of one of the *last* moments I shared with my students each year.

As clouds gathered over our small town the day before the *last* day of school, strong storms soon followed and our town began feeling the effects of tornadoes in the area. Students had been dismissed earlier in the day, and teachers were getting the *last* minute details completed before our *last* day of school. I finished the final touches and then headed home for the evening, hoping the storms would soon pass.

When I received the call that we would not be returning to see our children and enjoying the traditions of watching videos showing the fun and accomplishments, presenting award certificates, playing games, and parting for the adventures of the summer, my heart began to hurt. I realized that I would not have the opportunity to give those last *goodbyes*.

Those *last goodbyes* were not just a simple gesture for me. They symbolized my letting go of precious lives who had become such a part of me. During those hugs, I would tell each child how important he or she was, how proud I was of them, and that they could always come to me if they needed anything.

While we did have a day later for parents to bring children to pick up their belongings and awards, there were many who could not come. Those who could not come were, in my heart and mind, the ones who needed the *last hug and goodbye* the most.

Last goodbyes now hold an extremely important place on my agenda. Losing a loved one is one of the hardest of the *last goodbyes*. However, my experiences in May of 2016 taught me that as I proceed through each school year, I need to remember to initiate the hugs and reassurances on a regular basis so that I will not regret the absence of a *last goodbye*.

The end of that school year didn't happen as we had planned. It wasn't ideal. But even in the midst of chaos, you can learn some pretty important lessons.

———————

What's your usual reaction when chaos rears its head and something unexpected happens? When there's no closure? The answer is you simply do the best you can.

THINGS TO CONSIDER

- When have you had to show resilience in the face of unexpected adversity?
- How can you be prepared to handle the unexpected?

Tweet your answers and tell your story at #KidsDeserveIt

CHAPTER 12

SWITCH DAY

The one thing I have been reminded of again and again is the power of walking in someone else's shoes. To see the world from another person's perspective is to gain insight and understanding.

A few years ago, I worked under a principal who had us do a "Switch Day." It was an opportunity for us to switch classrooms with someone from another grade level for forty-five minutes, so we could get a glimpse into their daily life. I was terrified when I had to do this. I didn't know the kids or the curriculum, and I wasn't sure I could handle the grade level I had been assigned. But I love a challenge, and, honestly, it was one of the most fun assignments I had ever been given by my principal.

It made such an impact I decided to do "Switch Day" at Webb during my first year as principal. When I mentioned what was going to take place, I got three expected reactions. I got groans, excitement, and fear. But as we discussed it, the team's concerns began to ease a little. We can do anything for one hour, right?

I assigned every classroom teacher a switch partner—someone at least two grade levels away from their current grade. Sometimes a stigma can be attached to certain grade levels. Teachers working with older students think, "Look at those kindergarten teachers—they just get to play and paint and build all day. They don't comprehend the stress I'm under with these teenagers and their hormones and standardized testing!" And those kindergarten teachers say, "Those fifth grade teachers have it easy. Sure, they have that test to worry about, but at least they don't have to tie shoes all day, or answer a million questions every five minutes, or have someone in tears at least once a day."

A STORY FROM COURTNEY MOORE

Fifth Grade Teacher

Webb is an all-around special school, but one of my favorite things that was implemented my first year there was "Switch Day." I'm a fifth grade teacher at Webb, which is a pre-kindergarten through fifth grade school, so when I found out I was switching with a pre-kindergarten teacher, I couldn't help but be excited (and a little nervous at the same time).

The morning we switched, I decided to do some science experiments because I teach science. I started by asking my new four-year-old friends what they were learning about. They were so excited to tell me they were learning about the ocean. So I asked them if they knew the song "Baby Shark." Of course they did, so we sang it together! After our song, I did some experiments, and the kids kept yelling out, "It's magic!" It was so much fun to see them excited about school and learning. I showed them how acids and bases will turn water, with a universal indicator in it, either red or purple. Of course, I didn't use those words when explaining it to a four-year-old. They clapped and laughed, which really made it fun. I ended my "magic show" by creating elephant toothpaste, which they liked so much that, of course, we had to do it again.

I can honestly say, I had no reason to be nervous because four-year-olds are way less intimidating than eleven-year-olds—and way more welcoming short term. I had a class full of kids who thought I was so amazing for showing them neat "magic," and it only took forty-five minutes. I think the realization hit that they hadn't experienced quite as much hard life yet as my fifth grade class.

I appreciate what the pre-kindergarten, and now second grade teachers (my switch class from last year), do even more now than I did before because I have seen a glimpse into their everyday lives. I loved pre-kindergarten, but it takes A LOT of energy to keep up with them all day. I also appreciate that I can reason with my fifth graders, which isn't as easy with second graders or younger. "Switch Day" taught me how to walk a mile in another grade level's shoes, which is something every teacher should experience. It is something I will always take with me because it really made an impact.

The reality is every grade level has its trials and struggles. Every grade level also has its immense joys. Sometimes we don't know how great a certain grade or age can be until we've had the opportunity to spend some time with those students.

We did our first "Switch Day" in 2016, and it went really well. Teachers were buzzing everywhere about how much fun it was.

When I started sharing the experience, some people asked if the teachers had to plan lessons for the classroom they were entering. I left that decision to the switch partners. Most teachers left a lesson—as they would have for a sub—for the incoming teacher.

I loved walking by classrooms all day and seeing the teachers adapting to their new environments. My favorite was watching second grade and fifth grade teachers conducting second grade and fifth grade experiments in pre-kindergarten classes! Those kids ate up every second and learned some amazing vocabulary. When it was over, the teachers offered the following feedback:

"It was very fun!"

"Pre-K teachers are amazing! :-) I enjoyed pre-K way more than I thought I would! Thank you for this opportunity. My mom served as a pre-K teacher-director for years. I definitely have more appreciation for what she did on a daily basis. And I'm so thankful for our pre-K teachers."

"I truly enjoyed switching today. It was kind of like the TV show "Wife Swap." When I returned to my class, my students acted as if they had not seen me in a week! I had missed them as much as they had missed me, and it was only for an hour! The kinder students were fantastic, but I just missed my kids. There was nothing wrong with the teacher they had and my students all said they had a good time, but they missed me for some reason. It was great!"

"It was neat to interact with kids I do not usually see other than in the hallways or in the cafeteria. I loved being able to see how I could scaffold down activities to suit a lower grade. It was also interesting to see how I needed to adapt my management to a lower grade level as well. Very eye opening. I would suggest for next year doing one in the fall and one in the spring."

"I loved it!"

"Loved it!"

"While in the third grade classroom, I did not tie any shoes! If we do it next year, I would like to do it earlier in the year. I think January would be a good time."

"I liked it because it helped me appreciate the teacher I switched with and see what she deals with every day."

"I loved it. We got to plan the activity and the kids were excited to participate. The only thing I would change is the date because the last weeks of school are hectic."

Throughout the next school year, teachers asked on multiple occasions if "Switch Day" was coming back—and when. Some even requested grade levels they didn't have the year before.

And yes, even I took part in "Switch Day!" You have to be in the trenches with your team if you expect them to jump off that cliff with you. I took over a first grade classroom, and that teacher got to be the principal for an hour.

A STORY FROM BRENDA PARKER
Pre-Kindergarten Teacher

Not again! That's how I often look at the great ideas my principal comes up with. Why do I need to do something different? I am perfectly happy doing what I always do because I know it works. These words come out of my mouth quite often since I work with Todd Nesloney. And then I have to eat my words and tell him how great his ideas were because I always grow in the end. If you want to be a truly great teacher (or even human being), get comfortable with being uncomfortable. That's when you know you are on the verge of becoming all you were meant to be.

We can all learn something from walking in someone else's shoes. We can gain more respect, see a new angle, and maybe even fall in love with a grade level we never expected to enjoy.

Stepping out and working with new groups of children can be daunting. It can feel overwhelming and a little scary, but the deeper learning happens when we move outside our comfort zone.

THINGS TO CONSIDER

- How can you organize your own "Switch Day" with a friend?
- What have you done recently to push yourself outside your comfort zone?

Tweet your answers and tell your story at #KidsDeserveIt

CHAPTER 13

A SURPRISE FROM A PIRATE

Every chance I get, I talk about the power of social media. I tell people the value in getting connected, sharing their stories, and learning from and with others from around the world. And sometimes I get the eye rolls, the huffing and puffing, and the I'll-never-do-that comments.

But yet again, the first day of school this past school year was another example of why I choose to be a connected educator. It was a Monday, and we were as excited as we were ready because as I wrote in Chapter 11, we didn't get a last day of school with our kids at the end of the previous year.

A STORY FROM LISHA WORRALL AND ANDREA DAY

First Grade Teachers

At Webb Elementary, we are challenged and pushed to get our story out there, to share the good that we are doing with our kids, and to collaborate and make those connections on social media. On our first day of school last year, we did just that. We tweeted out all of the ice breakers and getting-to-know-you activities we were doing in our class rooms. We were sharing our excitement of the first day of school. What happened next left us speechless!

As we were getting our kids out to car riders that afternoon and starting to send them off, we looked up the drive and saw someone walking toward us. As we shielded our eyes from the sun, and the person got closer, we thought, *Surely not. This can't be right. We have to be delirious from the first day of school.* As the person got to us, we were right. DAVE BURGESS WAS STANDING THERE! Yes, you heard us correctly: DAVE BURGESS! Once the shock wore off and we could find our voices (and of course, after we snapped some super awesome pictures), Todd walked up to him, with a look of amazement and shock just like the rest of us, and asked what he was doing there. As it turns out, Dave was on his way to an event he had scheduled in Houston. As he drove down the highway, he saw a sign that said Navasota. He said, "Hey, I remember seeing

things from, and reading about, a school in Navasota on Twitter." He pulled over, looked it up, and decided to just drop on by!

This was an experience we will not soon forget! We learned
firsthand that day just how important it is to put your journey
of the classroom on social media. It gets you noticed, remembered, and you reach and inspire more than you think.

———

Let me just say, the first day was amazing. My team killed it.
They bonded with the kids, and there were smiles, hugs, and
high fives everywhere. Aside from a few arrival and dismissal
hiccups, it was a pretty perfect start to the school year.

But like Lisha and Andrea share above, the epic part came at
the very end of the day. You see, I do car rider duty every day. I
was outside, in the Texas heat, in the middle of two lanes of cars,
directing first-day traffic when out of nowhere, a guy walks up
to me. I immediately recognized him as Dave Burgess. Yes, *the*
Dave Burgess, the guy who wrote *Teach Like a Pirate*, the book
that changed my educational life. The guy who gave me my first
book deal. That guy.

The first words out of my mouth were, "What?! What are
you doing here?" I couldn't believe my eyes. It was one of those
moments when you're standing there thinking, *There's no way
I'm seeing what I'm seeing!*

The teachers were freaking out because they knew who he
was too. It turned out Dave was traveling through Texas, from
one city to another, and passed by a sign that said Navasota. He
knew I worked there, so he pulled over, looked up the address of
the school, and decided to do a surprise drop in.

It's also worth noting that I've known Dave for a little more than five years now. I started following Dave on social media because of his book, tweeting about it constantly while reading it because it was changing my perspective on so many things. Then I had the opportunity to be in San Diego, as I was getting recognized by the National School Board Association, and Dave saw my tweets about being there and asked to meet up. He took my wife and me out to dinner in San Diego, and I was in awe. It was one of my first real experiences of how walls could be torn down by being on social media.

That one dinner led to more meet-ups with Dave at several more conferences. We chatted over social media, talked on the phone, and forged a connection that resulted in him publishing my first full-fledged book, *Kids Deserve It!*, with Adam Welcome.

After getting over the shock that Dave Burgess was at my school, I begged him to stay about thirty minutes because we always do a quick we-survived-the-day staff meeting. Being Dave, he said yes and was able to meet my whole team and even share a magic trick or two.

I share this story primarily to show everyone what a great guy Dave is but also to show the power of being a connected educator. I never would have connected with Dave, much less had him surprise me at my school, if I hadn't taken that first leap on social media.

THINGS TO CONSIDER

- What can you do to surprise a friend today?
- How can you celebrate someone by surprising them on your campus tomorrow?

Tweet your answers and tell your story at #KidsDeserveIt

CHAPTER 14

EVERYONE MATTERS

As a classroom teacher, and now a principal, I've seen first-hand the important role every person plays in keeping a school running smoothly. For whatever reason, though, much of the public focus is on our classroom teachers and campus administrators. Too often, the arts teachers, instructional aides, nurses, librarians, special education teachers, cafeteria staff, custodial staff, and so many more are overlooked.

That has always bothered me.

A STORY FROM REBECCA (BECKY) MADISON
School Nurse

I am a registered nurse with a background of being the charge nurse in a recovery room at a large teaching hospital. I was blessed to acquire custody of my three granddaughters ten years ago. I retired from the hospital, and we moved to Waller, Texas, to put the girls in a better school district. I met Todd Nesloney at that time. He was my oldest granddaughter's teacher. When he was asked to be the principal in Navasota, I convinced him he could not live without me as his school nurse. Now, we've just finished our third year together.

Being a school nurse is the most rewarding job I have ever had. While at the hospital, I was responsible for saving lives, but as the school nurse, I would like to think I am making a difference in the lives of all of our students. I not only take care of their health needs, but I also love and nurture them every day. We have our "frequent flyers," as we call them, who make multiple visits—sometimes on the same day—to the clinic. I tend to attract needy students, and I challenge myself with the more difficult cases. I hear all kinds of stories of how injuries have happened and the imaginations of these young people lighten my heart.

My goal is for our kiddos to remember Mrs. Madison as the best school nurse ever. I also want them to know they are loved and special and that they matter. I believe God put me exactly where I am supposed to be.

When I first read this account from our school nurse, it was a good reminder of her contribution to Webb Elementary. What Becky failed to write, because she's just that kind of person, is how much of herself she pours into her job. On a weekly basis, she asks permission to go to Wal-Mart to use her own money to buy shoes, shorts, food, and toys to help fill the needs some of our students have. And let me tell you, a school nurse doesn't make a ton of money. Becky can often be found in my office, sharing her concerns about students and checking to see if we know why they weren't at school today. There are few educators I have met with hearts as big as hers. Becky and her equally amazing assistant, Brittany Taylor, organize blood drives, clothing drives, food drives, our lost and found, and even help cover classrooms when we're shorthanded. Why do they go to so much trouble? One reason is it's simply who they are. Another is they know our kids deserve to have a caring adult involved in their lives. Our kids deserve people they can count on.

A STORY FROM HAVEN WISNOSKI

Librarian

Growing up, I always said that I wanted to move far away from where I grew up and that I would never work or live in a small town—and especially not my hometown. Well, guess what? I ended up marrying a hometown boy and was blessed with the opportunity to teach at my former elementary school. This gave me the chance to work alongside some of the teachers that I looked up to as a child . . . the teachers who inspired me to teach! I started out teaching kindergarten and stayed there for twelve years. I taught first grade for a year while I was working on my masters of library science degree, and this is my twelfth year as the librarian—all at John C. Webb Elementary.

Teaching in the same place for so long has provided me the privilege of getting to know each child extremely well and has given me the opportunity to form unique bonds with them and their families. I've been able to witness firsthand their successes as well as their failures, whether it be through tears of happiness or sadness in academics, sports, extracurricular activities, or other life-changing events, such as graduating, marriage, starting a family, criminal activity, or even death. Each and every student holds a very special place in my heart! I try to instill in my students the knowledge that they will always have their own personal support system or cheering squad no matter the situation at any given time in their lives.

I have developed a sense of fulfillment, like that of a mom, to so many students over the years. My heart swells with love and pride when I get to see my former students in action, working in various places around town, or when I see them with their kids walking into the school every day. I love how their kid's face lights up when I tell them stories of when their mom and dad were in school. I especially enjoy seeing Facebook posts with photos and messages from former students and their family members.

When I left the classroom for the library, it changed my world. I was able to teach all 700+ students each and every day! Nowadays, it doesn't matter where, when, or what time of day it may be, it never fails that I run into current or former students and their families when I'm out and about in town. At times I feel like a movie star or royalty being swarmed by a flash mob, and it's the greatest feeling in the world. So I encourage you to try to stay in one place for as long as you can, no matter if it's big or small, your hometown or not—you won't be disappointed with the memories and relationships you will create.

At Webb I also have the pleasure of lunch duty every day. I love getting to talk to the men and women who serve our children their meals. I enjoy hearing about their struggles, laughing at their joyful memories, and so much more. My favorite part is getting behind the counter to serve food alongside them. Not only does it show your team that you're not too important to do any job, it also gives you the opportunity to appreciate the cafeteria staff in a personal way. The head of the cafeteria staff let me know that all her staff had to go online and take a course to be able to serve food, so I couldn't just jump back there. I paid the fifteen-dollar fee, took a two-hour course, and passed the test, which wasn't as easy as you'd think!

That next day, I wore the gloves and hairnet and served our kids their lunches. You should have seen their shocked faces. I hoped I was sending a powerful message to my students that we step up and do every job. No one is better than anyone else. And in all honesty, I had a great time working with our cafeteria staff and developed a greater appreciation of what they do every single day.

A STORY FROM MAURA PAVLOCK
Special Education Aide

Instructional Aides (IAs) are a hidden asset in our school. In some schools they're not always treated with respect.

I first worked with a teacher who actually taught me that my self-worth was worth more than any college degree she could ever earn. She came to me after a few months of employment and told me, along with the other two aides, "You can go get a job as a Wal-Mart greeter, but I have my master's!" I haven't always been one to bite my tongue, but I am glad that I did that day. Nothing good would have come out of what I wanted to say, and today I can say I am stronger and still working magic with these babies.

I am embarking on my tenth year with the Preschool Program for Children with Disabilities (PPCD) at Webb. Wow. Ten years, four different teachers, and two principals. I remember walking into this school, new to this small town, and new to a small town, period. I have traveled most of my life, so coming to Navasota and settling down was a welcome change.

Funny thing is, I have always worked with and loved on those with special needs. Never thought anything about it. Got married and prayed for healthy children like all mothers do. When my oldest was eleven and my youngest was five, I interviewed for the instructional aide position in PPCD. My interview was awesome, so I got to go observe where I was working. I was in love. I never looked back on that decision. I have always loved working with and playing with children. All children!

Seeing my students progress in PPCD, all their hard-won accomplishments, was worth every pay raise I never got. My first child, the reason I was hired, was a little boy. Oh, did he capture my heart from the get-go! His family said he could talk, but he never did with us. After several months, I was changing and talking to him. I always talked to my kiddos everywhere. He said, "You're ugly!" It stopped me dead in my tracks. What did I just hear? I looked at him and asked, "What did you say?" He started laughing, and so did I. Then he said it again. "You're ugly!" Then both of us busted out in hysterics. I was in tears, and I called the teacher and had him tell her, and this time that little stinker said, "Ms. P is ugly!" Those words were the best words I have ever heard!

Another of my little girls came in with hearing aids. Her mom was frustrated because she kept taking them off and losing them—on purpose. As time went on, I shared with this little girl that I also wore hearing aids. I told her I would never not want to wear them because I know what I am missing out on. It took a little encouragement and convincing, but she eventually stopped 'losing' her hearing aids!

And yet another student, a little girl with Down Syndrome, would always sing herself to sleep, and to this day I still hear her humming in my memories of her.

I believe instructional aides are a vital part of any school and should be valued for the work they do to keep classrooms running smoothly.

Everyone on our campus plays an important role. No single person makes a bigger impact than anyone else. What truly makes the difference is how much we care about the students we serve. They need all of us—the custodian sharing life lessons with the kids he passes in the hallway, the librarian recommending a book that gives a child hope, and the music teacher whose smile boosts the spirits of the student struggling to hold on.

Every single person on a campus matters. It's important that we take the time to truly show our appreciation and remind others of their worth and what they bring to the table.

THINGS TO CONSIDER

- Who on your campus could you take time to celebrate a little more?

- Think of the people who have made a huge impact on your educational career. What have they done for you and what would you like to say to them?

Tweet your answers and tell your story at #KidsDeserveIt

CHAPTER 15

THE LIGHT AND THE DARK

The metaphor of darkness and light has always been a powerful one for me. It's that whole idea that darkness seems all encompassing, even suffocating. You can't escape it, and its weight is so heavy. Then, with even the tiniest spark or flame, darkness runs.

Light clears the way. Those images come to mind when I reflect on our jobs as teachers. There can be a lot of darkness in our profession—looming deadlines, overwhelming workloads and expectations, upset parents, disobedient kids, difficult co-workers. Sometimes that darkness feels overwhelming.

In those moments, when darkness surrounds us, we must choose to be the light. We must choose to be the spark that grows into a flame, driving the darkness away. We have to find a hope we can cling to, people who will lift us up instead of dragging us down, and the strength within ourselves to do the same for others.

A STORY FROM JANE BREWER

Math Interventionist

 The scar is so fresh that it's not totally a scar; there are still flecks of scab. About an inch long and a quarter of an inch wide, it lies midway up my left arm. Small, innocuous, not anything you would ever ask about, it is a symbol—a symbol of how the love of man fails you and the love of God never does. A symbol that I have a purpose on the earth and a task to achieve. A symbol that I matter.

Have you ever said, "I feel like I've been hit by a truck?" Well, I actually was.

A Ford F-150 clipped my arm while I was cycling on a dark country road. The headlight on my bike had malfunctioned, and I was using the flashlight feature on my cell phone. I never blacked out, as the EMTs kept asking me, but it certainly seemed that I got from the grass to the ambulance in seconds. One of the questions the police asked me was how fast I thought that truck was going. I said forty miles per hour.

In retrospect, that was ridiculous. The speed limit was fifty-five, and he was passing another car. He was going sixty miles per hour at least. Because I was so far to the right, his left mirror barely clipped my arm as he passed. It caused a small cut and a severe bruise but did no other damage. The chiropractor I saw that afternoon (I already had the appointment, so I just kept it.) said my back wasn't even out of alignment. How many people do you know who have gotten hit by a Ford F-150 going sixty miles per hour and *walked away*?

I had been praying for a miracle of God in a complex relationship. The man I thought I loved and who I thought loved me was on a pilgrimage in Spain, deciding his future and whether we had one together. I told him about the truck, and he barely reacted; and in every conversation we have had since, he has NEVER asked about my arm. I work nights tutoring at a local college, and I have a student who asks about my arm every time he sees me. We aren't lovers. We aren't even friends. He is just a decent human being. Some people can see when they're in a bad relationship. Others need to be hit by a truck.

It was three days later that I realized I had gotten my miracle. It was another day before I realized what it meant. God loves me. He loves me so much He preserved my life in a situation where I could have died. He has a purpose for me I have not yet achieved. (I'm a little nervous about that. Once I've achieved it, will it be "bring on the trucks?")

And so I sometimes caress that small innocuous little scar and remember God's love. I remember to look for my purpose. I remember I matter.

Sometimes in order to be the light, we have to go through our own darkness to find it. I love Jane's story above about how she re-found her own light in the midst of what could have been a deadly accident.

Another important way we are the light is with the words we share online. A family member came up to me a few weeks ago to vent about "all you people in education." She told me, "I can't stand when I see a teacher complaining about something on Facebook. They chose that career, they work with kids, for goodness' sake. If I were to complain about something in my job, my boss would call me and write me up or fire me, but I see it from teachers all the time."

That really hit me. Most weeks I see teachers from all over the country complaining about their jobs on Facebook. "The kids were crazy today." "I felt so disrespected at work." "I hate all this paperwork. Why can't I just teach?" And guess what? Those are real and valid complaints. They are. But think of the negative energy we're putting out into the world at large when we get on social media and complain about teaching the children in our communities. Or worse yet, what about when we hear these conversations in the hallways or teachers' lounges of our schools? In the checkout line at the grocery store? What kind of message are we sending? How would you feel, as a parent, if you saw your child's teachers complaining about all they have to do to take care of your child? We can't forget that there are always little eyes watching and little ears listening. They hear us even when we were sure we were quiet enough not to be heard.

We must think twice about what we choose to post and the words we use, even when the day has been a doozy. As educators, whether it's fair or not, we're held to a higher standard. We've been given a gift by being entrusted with the minds of little ones, and we can't forget that. Let's make sure we're spreading light, not darkness.

THINGS TO CONSIDER

- Have you ever posted a comment online or said something in the hallway or teachers' lounge about a student or colleague that you later regretted? What did you learn from the experience?

- How can you continually be a light in an often dark world?

Tweet your answers and tell your story at #KidsDeserveIt

CHAPTER 16

I WILL NOT BE SILENT

In January 2017, the Texas Education Agency (TEA) released information on a new Texas Rating System. It's a very simplified system that gives every school and district in Texas ratings on an A–F scale. Although this system was originally not officially going to go into effect until August 2018, the state released preliminary ratings to the public at large in January of 2017.

If you followed the news leading up to that announcement, you probably remember scores of educators voicing disdain for the new system. For the first time in all my years in education, I saw districts rising up with one voice to stand against this injustice.

What's the injustice, you might ask?

In my opinion, the injustice is the wholesale misunderstanding of education.

There has been much research released on the reality that schools with a higher population of minority and impoverished families score lower than their counterparts. Some of that research shows that if you remove the standardized testing from the equation completely, you could figure out school ratings based on minority groups and socioeconomic status alone.

And that's the problem. The people who are making decisions concerning our schools and our students have often never stepped foot into a public education classroom since the days they themselves were students (if as students, they even attended a public school to begin with).

So how does this happen? It's partly because of us. We educators haven't stood together and spoken out against these short-sighted policies. Not enough of us have called legislators, written letters, or marched to our state capitals. We complain, we say lawmakers are failing us, but we haven't done enough to make them truly understand the problem. And I'm tired of not doing enough. I'm ready to do more, and this year I'm pledging to use my voice to speak.

Why now? Because our schools are so much more than a single A–F rating. Out of four domains, my campus, Webb Elementary, received three F ratings and one C. How does that make a parent or community member feel? How does that make our kids feel? What about the teachers who are showing up every day busting their butts to give our students a high-quality education? Speaking for myself, as someone who knows the great work we do, the F ratings cut deep. It hurts because those grades are not reflective of the strides we are making at Webb, but those scores are out there in the public conversation.

In my opinion, this new rating system falls short because it doesn't take into account some of the harder-to-measure successes that Webb and many others schools are experiencing. It doesn't measure the progress we've made in connecting with families. It doesn't measure that we've had more than 350 families attend our Hot Dog Cookout at a local apartment complex every semester. Nor does it measure that we had more than 580 men come to our two Dinner with a Gentleman events with their child. It doesn't show how excited our students are to come to school. It doesn't measure those children we have connected with and helped find success in an area for the first time in their lives. The new rating system doesn't take into account the $500 our school nurse spent from her own pocket to buy students deodorant, toothpaste, or even clothes because the children couldn't afford it themselves and were too embarrassed to ask for it.

It doesn't show the excitement our students have for our new "house system"—from the Ron Clark Academy—that has brought everyone together, emphasized teamwork, and helped kids learn character traits and grow into better citizens. It doesn't measure the pride of the child who spent the entire day in her kindergarten classroom without hitting another student because she's been working with her teacher on self-control. Those ratings don't reflect the little boy who regularly cries in the front office, begging to stay with one of us because he doesn't want to go home for the weekend. It doesn't measure the lessons he learns as we console him and teach him how to live through difficult circumstances.

This new rating system doesn't value our many teachers who spend hours each week attending Little League football, baseball, soccer, and T-Ball games. Or dance recitals, kickboxing competitions, or cheer and gymnastics events. It doesn't register that we've decreased our in-school suspension and out-of-school suspension rates by more than 90 percent in less than a year because we've been teaching students how to manage their emotions and react with respect. Or what about the love of reading we have instilled in our students? What about the new culture of reading we've created where teachers are advertising what they're reading and students are sharing book recommendations on campus, checking out library books at unprecedented rates, and reading during dismissal and arrival simply because they want to?

The A–F rating system doesn't value our counselor's work with many different families this Christmas season to surprise them with groceries or presents so they could celebrate the season with a little less stress. It doesn't consider the countless CPS calls, parent counseling, drug and alcohol lessons/counseling, or sexual abuse that we help kids and families work through. It doesn't celebrate our innovative teachers who are trying flexible seating, classroom transformations, cross grade-level collaborations, lessons with Olympic athletes, Skype calls with classes from across the world, and so much more.

No, the new rating system judges us on one test. A single day in the lives of kids dealing with all kinds of chaos. Does it take into consideration that two of our students had trouble focusing because they were dealing with their father being shot the night before in a fight over drugs? No. Does it value the work we've done to help third graders who are overwhelmed by their dread of the state exam? No. What about the immense stress our teachers feel as they fight to rise above that F rating—even though they know they are doing their best? No.

Texas' new rating system is demeaning to teachers and families. It puts extra pressure on school boards and superintendents to fix their low-performing schools.

But how do I convince my teachers they are doing a great job of filling in the gaps when the state has told them their school is failing? How do I make our parents understand their children's school is truly changing lives when the state has said it doesn't measure up? How do I make our students understand they are not the cause of our low test scores—that they are inquisitive, bright, energetic, world-changing kids who, despite the challenges they face at home, come to school every day ready to learn?

It's a daily battle to remind myself and my team that we are not defined by our performance on a one-size-fits-all standardized exam. But I will fight on and encourage others to join the effort. We have to speak up and share the greatness that goes on in our schools—especially when the state deems us a failure. We must rise up and show up every day to give our kids and parents the best education they could hope for.

When you work in communities overcome by poverty, you realize the damage these ratings can do. But I will not be silent. I will no longer complain behind school walls or in small groups of educators. What I will do is shout from the rooftops and in every forum I can find about the incredible work my team does on a daily basis. I will write and call my state legislators and march to Austin if I have to.

Closer to home, I will remind my students they are wonderful, that they are more than any test score will ever tell them they are. I will praise my team for the wonderful work they do and assure them the countless hours they put in are not wasted. I will continually share with our parents how hard their children and our school staff are working to give their children the best education possible.

Will you join me?

THINGS TO CONSIDER

- In what ways can you stand up and use your voice for your students and their education?
- What are some of the successes happening in your classroom or school that aren't valued by your state's testing system?

Tweet your answers and tell your story at #KidsDeserveIt

CHAPTER 17

WE CAN ALL GROW

Something I talk about quite often is that educators must continually find ways to grow. In *Kids Deserve It!*, one of my favorite lines is, "How dare we walk into our schools every day and tell our students to learn if we ourselves aren't learning."

We must be open to personal growth as well. Not one of us has reached that pinnacle of knowing everything, though sometimes we—yes, me too—like to act as if we have.

A STORY FROM JULIE BROOKS
Pre-Kindergarten Teacher

When Mr. Nesloney asked me to teach pre-kindergarten, I did not know what to think. My teaching experience had always been in the third and fourth grades. I trusted his judgment, however, and I was determined to show him I could take on this new challenge in my teaching career. Little did I know that I would end up finding a new love and passion for the path he placed in front of me.

People often ask me what it is that I love about my job. The quick answer is that these kids come to my classroom with such innocence and an excitement for learning. They are eager to discover new things. I quickly learned that it goes much deeper than that, though. At Webb, pre-kindergarten is their first experience in a big school. In our classroom, we learn both academics and a love of a school and classroom family. Some days we are at the top of our game and everything goes as planned. Lesson plans are completed, and everyone is happy. Some days are tough. Some days I feel like the only thing we accomplish is wiping tears and giving countless hugs. I had to realize that both kinds of days are a success. What seemed like our bad days really weren't bad at all. We were learning what it was like to be a part of something bigger. We were learning to be a family.

We have our ups and downs but most importantly, we are still learning and growing through triumphs and failures. This is why I love my job. I am still learning as much as my students are. They are teaching me as much as I am teaching them. When you take a look in our classroom, you will see that we love, support, and encourage one another. Not only are we Mrs. Brooks' pre-kindergarten class in room 402, we are much bigger. We are the future!

I so clearly remember having that conversation with Julie about moving down to pre-kindergarten. I felt like it was where she was meant to be, even though she couldn't see it herself. Leaders sometimes have to make those difficult calls that are hard for others to understand. I also remember talking to Susan Brak.

Susan had been teaching as an interventionist for many years before our district, due to some budgeting concerns, eliminated those positions, pushing Susan back into the classroom as a kindergarten teacher.

A STORY FROM SUSAN BRAK

Reading and Dyslexia Interventionist

Teaching is full of challenges. I began my teaching career teaching third grade for one year. Then I ended up teaching kindergarten for the next eleven years and absolutely loved it. Then I was blessed with the opportunity to teach first grade struggling readers utilizing Reading Recovery. As our growing district began to make some changes, I became a part of our reading intervention and dyslexia programs teaching kindergarten through third grade. It was very fulfilling and difficult at the same time. Teaching individual students and small groups allows you to focus on each child's strengths and weaknesses. Every child is unique in personality, learning style, background, and ability. Over the years, I constantly receive reminders that every child is unique and that you cannot judge a book by its cover. A child can seem that he has every opportunity he needs to be successful and still be at risk of failure. Being a teacher means being a learner because you have to constantly learn more and more about your students so that you can help them become the best they can be.

Recently, it was a time of major changes for our district. Webb was transitioning from a pre-K through third grade campus to a pre-K through fifth grade campus. After nineteen years as an interventionist, I once again was asked to move back into the classroom as a kindergarten teacher. Now, I am a flexible person, but this was going to be a real shift. Many challenges and blessings occurred as I made this transition back into the classroom after being a small group instructor for so many years. As I received my list of students, I became very excited about providing these students the foundation they needed to be successful. At Meet the Teacher Night, I realized that one of my students was the daughter of a former kindergarten student—one of the treasures of teaching many years in the same district. It was such a blessing to see this mother having high hopes for her daughter. The daughter left kindergarten being a great reader and mathematician because her parents had believed in her so much. Being a more experienced teacher, I believe that I was able to truly appreciate each kindergarten student's uniqueness and build upon it. Some wanted to share all of their verbal knowledge with everyone else, while others just wanted to sit quietly and observe. Each student brought something special to our class. We had many strong personalities, which will help these students be a success. As a kindergarten teacher, it was my job to help each child to develop his strong personality to overcome learning difficulties. It was truly a blessing to be back in the kindergarten classroom for that year.

Many things have changed since I was in the classroom in the 1990s, but kids are still kids. They want and need acceptance, boundaries, guidance, exercise, music, poetry, phonemic awareness, phonics, reading, math exploration, science, books, crayons, computers, and more.

I am now back in the reading interventionist and dyslexia position, but that kindergarten class of 2015–2016 will always hold a very special place in my heart! They are a group of amazing people with a variety of personalities and each one is a wonderful treasure.

———

Part of my job is to work with teachers to help them grow. My admin team and I send them to and bring in various forms of professional development. We do walk-throughs of their class, sit with some of them one-on-one, push them into new environments and teaching strategies, and use the T-TESS (Texas Teacher Evaluation and Support System) process to help us along the way.

T-TESS is our new state system for evaluating teachers. It is a very intensive process on the administrators' end, but it provides great feedback and is truly a powerful, reflective system if used the way it was designed.

Sometimes professional growth is uncomfortable, sometimes it's fun, and sometimes it's hard and makes teachers want to cry or walk away. But I never want to ask my team to do something I wouldn't do myself. That's why I'm passionate about reading to classes, doing morning, lunch, and afternoon duty, helping plan lessons, team teaching, modeling lessons, sitting in professional learning communities (PLCs), working with our state-provided instructional coach, and more. I do that because I, myself, also have a lot of growing to do. I make it a point to do a self-inventory every week to remind myself of things to work on. One of the most dangerous phrases in education is, "We've always done it that way." Another one is, "What I'm already doing is working better than everything else. Why do I need to grow?"

One way I've tried to explore professional growth with my team is through our Swivl Recordings. About two years ago, we purchased a Swivl robot, a powerful tool to have in any classroom. One year my team and I completed all of our teacher evaluations before Christmas, and we wanted to continue the growth process during January. So we recorded every teacher for thirty minutes, and the teacher watched their recordings and submitted written reflections of what they observed, noting how they were addressing the two areas of refinement we identified in their December evaluations.

Recording yourself is daunting, but watching the recording is downright scary. Personally, I hate hearing my voice and seeing myself move. But when I did it—during my fifth year of teaching—it was really helpful. I learned that I said "um" way too much, and that, for some reason, I taught to the left side of the room 70 percent of my instructional time. I'd had no idea!

Because we asked our teachers to do it, my team and I felt we needed to do the same. So we spent two weeks going into different classrooms and recording ourselves teaching a lesson. It was even more nerve wracking recording myself teaching as a principal. I wanted to be fantastic, but in full honesty, I wasn't pleased with my performance. But I learned from the experience. After all, that's the point—to model, learn, evolve, and improve.

Our next step, taken during our staff meeting that month, was for teachers to choose which administrator lesson they wanted to watch. Using T-TESS, they rated us! Yes, their administrators! Then my team and I spent the rest of the spring semester working on our areas of refinement as identified by our teachers. It was a truly humbling and exciting endeavor that every administrator should take part in. We need more instructional leaders and fewer campus managers.

A STORY FROM AARON MARVEL
Former Assistant Principal

Without the prospect of growth, ambitions evaporate, motivation diminishes, learning stops, and our lives begin to lose the luster of a hopeful and brighter future. A belief in the power and possibility of growth, after all, lies at the core of our reason for teaching; why would we teach without the belief that others can and should grow in knowledge, wisdom, and character? With that being said, if we as teachers believe in the power and possibility of growth, then we must also model the requisite behaviors that precede growth: transparency, reflection, and modification. Here at Webb Elementary, we do in fact believe that all students, teachers, AND administrators can and should learn and grow. For this reason, we have incorporated an uncomfortable but beautifully effective personalized learning approach in teacher video recordings.

Video recordings have placed transparency at the forefront of our growth model. Before anyone can make steps toward mastery, they must first know where they currently are in the learning process. As uncomfortable as it may be, a teacher watching a video of himself teaching places areas of reinforcement front and center. Identifying areas of needed growth alone, however, does not translate into improvement, but must be followed by time for deep and honest reflection. During this reflection process, teachers ask themselves where they are, where they are going, and most importantly, how they will get there. A plan of action begins to manifest, and the modification process can then begin. With time and a consistent cyclical process of transparency, reflection, and modification, teachers can experience great leaps in improvement, which most importantly translates into student success.

In addition, our video recording approach was completely made possible by our use of the Swivl robot. In a nutshell, a Swivl allows an individual to record without a cameraman. The Swivl base tracks a marker worn around the educator's neck, ensuring the person is always in view of the camera. The marker also records audio, guaranteeing the educator's voice can be clearly heard. After audio and video have been recorded, the file is easily uploaded to a private YouTube channel. The video link is shared with educators, who can easily watch their recorded lesson from the convenience of any device, whether at home or at work.

We have used the Swivl on our campus in two ways: (1) video learning teams and (2) campus-wide video reflections.

Video Learning Teams (VLTs): I first learned of VLTs from *Focus on Teaching: Using Video for High-Impact Instruction*, a book by Jim Knight, pioneer and advocate for the instructional coach approach. Simply put, VLTs are groups of teachers who agree to review one another's recorded lessons and provide feedback. I first presented this idea on our campus as an option for growth. I was pleased to have ten of our forty teachers sign up to participate. I created three groups, and the process was simple: (1) record the first teacher's lesson using the Swivl Robot, (2) share the video with the recorded teacher, (3) the recorded teacher watches his or her video and provides two or three big "look fors" to give the group an area on which to focus their feedback, (4) share the video with the other group members who then take notes and prepare for feedback, and (5) the group meets to watch any important parts of the lesson to help shed light on practice, and feedback is shared. The process is repeated with the remaining teachers within the group.

Campus Wide Video Reflections: Because we believe in the power of video reflection so much on our campus, we actually made it a requirement for each teacher to be recorded at least once during the school year. Establishing this requirement set off several alarms in our staff, so to show teachers how serious we were about having a growth mindset during this experience, all three administrators also were recorded while teaching a lesson. To calm teachers' fears, we set a rule that only the person being recorded would ever see the video unless they explicitly asked someone else to watch it. In fact, only two people ever had access to the video at any given time: myself, who recorded the video using the Swivl, and the recorded teacher. Setting this rule set minds at ease even further. Simply recording teachers, however, would not lead to a direct realization of areas of needed growth or to subsequent action. To encourage the growth process further, the teachers were required to write a short reflection about their personal strengths and weaknesses within the lesson, rate themselves in their area of refinement from our teacher appraisal system, and identify specific actions that would be taken to address the areas of needed growth. Lastly, each teacher shared the reflection with his or her appraiser, and followed up with a one-on-one meeting to further reflect and create an action plan.

As educators, we all desperately want to be effective because we care about our students, and we know much of their success hinges on our effectiveness as professionals. Providing educators with personalized learning opportunities, such as video recordings, can place the ownership of growth in the hands of the teachers, and, if used effectively, improve teacher motivation and satisfaction as they see themselves grow in their own practice.

Using strategies such as these can sometimes be uncomfortable, but I leave you with this quote: "Life begins at the end of your comfort zone." True growth and change require a little bit of discomfort, but the lives you will impact will be worth all the effort.

Growth is something we all should embrace, so let's remember to keep learning, keep improving. As professional educators, it's when we go through a trial or experience failure and *don't* use it as a lesson to learn that we run the risk of becoming complacent.

A STORY FROM OLIVIA AGUIÑAGA

Third Grade Teacher

I always knew I wanted to be in Navasota. I remember still having a year to go before I graduated from SHSU when I got a call to come meet with the then-principal at the old John C. Webb Elementary. I was immediately offered a position and signed my contract as a bilingual second grade teacher. From there on, it has been an experience each year.

Even though I wasn't in my early twenties like most new teachers, I felt young at work, working with teachers who had been there for many years. I was able to learn so much from wonderful teachers who had great experience and teachers who had been with the district for a long time. I even got to be on the same team as my second grade teacher. Who would have thought I would be working side by side with the same second grade teacher I had as a child, after all these years? I loved what I was doing and had gained a new family. I was also newly married and working till 7:00 p.m. every night. But this only lasted a year because the following year, we moved to a new school. I still remember us only having one weekend to move into a new building and start school that following Monday! Boy, that was a busy weekend.

With the move, it was like I was starting a new experience, a new school, new teachers, a new principal, and a baby on the way. Whew. I again worked with second grade for another six years and really enjoyed it, even though at times I felt I was missing something. Many times I wondered if I should have tried another district.

Just when I was getting comfortable, there came another change. I was getting moved to third grade three days, yes three days, before I went on maternity leave with my second child. I cried and cried because I didn't want to move to third grade. But my principal kept reassuring me that he felt like I belonged there and that I would be great! And you know what? I did fall in love with it. This move was what I was missing. I was able to see my students grow even more, and it seemed so much more challenging. Now being in a "state tested" grade level, it gave me what I needed. Once again, I began to gain a family with teachers around me, a place where I belonged. I felt life was perfect. Moving to another district was no longer an option with now having my own children.

But living in a small town, everyone knows you. I've built some great relationships with parents and students, and being bilingual has given me the opportunity to connect with even more. There are families who I've taught every single one of their children. I still remember when a parent called and said her son wanted me to be their godmother for their first communion. I always also find it funny when a parent calls and asks me to fuss at their child for not doing what they're supposed to at home. It makes me feel special that parents can come to me with their problems. I always tell my parents whatever you need, I'm here; I don't care what time you text me.

These next seven years were my best years as a teacher. I gained so much and created so many memories, not just with students but also with teachers. I literally felt like a kid in school having fun and creating times I would never forget. Memories that stick. Things like music playing in the hallway and all of third grade running out in the hallway and just dancing their hearts out for five minutes, or field day water balloon fights with teachers, or Fifties Day, and so much more. During spring break, my third grade team would even come up to the school to decorate our hallway, so our kids knew we meant business and it was time to work hard. Our principal at the time would even have us create an ornament at Christmas, depending on a theme, and decorate a tree in the foyer. There were even prizes for best ornament! I often think back on the many times I complained about things we were asked to do, but looking back now, I'm so thankful. The things we did and the fun we had just didn't feel like I was coming to work. I guess it's not something you could understand if you weren't at Webb.

The campus was very united, but we underwent so many changes with the state test, STAAR, and our curriculum that the scores of our students began to drop. We believed we could make it and get our kids where they needed to be, and man, we worked so HARD that year. And we were so pumped; all the other grade levels were super supportive. We were doing things we didn't have to or weren't being told to do, but instead things we wanted to. Then I remember our scores coming in and they called all the third grade teachers to the meeting room . . . and then there were tears, and nobody could speak. We missed the mark. We only needed fewer than ten more kids to pass for us to reach our state accountability rating.

There was another change. Our school went through reconstitution. Many teachers left, afraid, not knowing what was going to happen. That year was the most difficult year in my entire teaching career. It was so hard losing not just teachers but also friends I had made over the years. We all cared so much about these kids, yet we had to interview for our jobs, and prove why we should be allowed to stay. Our school also changed principals (that's when Nesloney came on board) and instead of it being a pre-kindergarten through third grade school, it became a pre-kindergarten through fifth grade campus.

What I've learned and been reminded of is that this is really where I belong. And even though the road hasn't been easy, I'm thankful for all the experiences I have been through. I now have two girls in our school, and I have been more than happy to keep them on the same campus as me. Many teachers have come and gone, but I'm still here. I don't like to think of myself as an old teacher, but instead as a teacher who has experience. There have been countless other teachers I have learned from who have helped shape me into who I am today. I am thankful to have become a teacher in a community where I live. A school where I went to school and where my girls are now attending. The road isn't easy, but learning never is, and I know that Webb Elementary is exactly where I'm meant to be.

THINGS TO CONSIDER

- What tool can you use to record yourself and then learn from the video?
- How are you choosing to grow on a daily basis?

Tweet your answers and tell your story at #KidsDeserveIt

CHAPTER 18

BE DIFFERENT

One of the things I love about working at Webb Elementary is how willing my team is to take risks and do something outside of the norm.

As a classroom teacher, I was always pushing boundaries. I wanted to be different, do the unexpected, and give my students new experiences. When teaching fifth grade, I had the idea of doing something fun as a last-minute detox before we took our state test. I planned a *Survivor*-themed relay race, dressed up like Jeff Probst, and even created a banner. We didn't vote anyone off the island, but we did have twelve stations where students had to work in groups to do everything from eating crackers and then singing "The Star-Spangled Banner" to solving riddles while hula hooping, to learning the latest dance craze in order to move forward in the race. It was an opportunity to just connect with my students, build teamwork, and offer up some stress relief, all at the same time.

A STORY FROM ALLISON GUY
Former Third Grade Teacher

In a classroom of wiggle worms, I decided that giving up fifteen minutes during the day would give me back about an hour of learning time. In the world of an underperforming campus, yielding a forty-five-minute gain sounded like bliss!

These were my expectations: By eight o'clock in the morning, the students would line up, and we would go outside to walk around the school and talk. The only rule was they had to stop at the corners, and they had to be able to see Ms. Calkins, my partner teacher, or me at all times. They could run, skip, hop, and talk—whatever they wanted as long as they didn't disturb the other classes.

I was worried the parents would give me some pushback because the students were losing fifteen minutes of academic instruction time. Much to my surprise, every parent was supportive and encouraging. The first day was chaos! It was like herding cats, but we survived. The next day wasn't nearly as crazy. By the following week, it was a part of our normal routine that the kids had come to expect and enjoy.

One of the best parts was having guest walkers. On Fridays, we'd invite the parents. We also had about eleven Navasota staff members, including our superintendent, join us. That support was immeasurable.

My teaching partner and I saw tremendous gains in the classroom. After the first week, the kids' attention spans soared. They were more engaged and willing to participate during class. We also saw improved attendance rates. Even the students who were chronic tardies started to set their own alarm clocks. On rainy days, we would walk around the school or do indoor athletic activities.

Looking back, if I could change one thing about our movement activities, it would be starting earlier in the year. Because of our morning walks, I have been able to get to know my students better, and they confide in us and tell us more about their lives. The benefits have far outweighed the loss of instructional time.

Another time I tried to think differently was after I found *Wreck This Journal* by Keri Smith. It was a fantastic little book with each page filled with ways to wreck the actual journal. Everything from "tie it to your bike and ride a half-mile down the road" to "eat your favorite candy and lick this page" to "draw outside this given circle." It was wild, it was crazy, but most of all, it was creative and fun. I took it with me everywhere to complete all the challenges. I couldn't get enough!

After realizing how much fun I was having, I really wanted to get a copy for all of our fourth graders. But like most second-year teachers, I was broke. So I bought a copy for all six members of my grade-level team to see if they would even be on board. They loved it as much as I did. I kept brainstorming ways to get every child a copy and finally decided to email the author. I explained the population of students I served, how I came across her book, the creativity it was inspiring in me, and how I wanted to use it to inspire the kids. I humbly inquired if she would be able to provide some sort of discount because we needed more than 125 copies and definitely couldn't afford them at full price.

After hearing my story, Smith was so moved that she did more than just give us a discount. She wrote a blog post on her website about our school and how I reached out to her because I wanted to use her book to inspire creativity in my students. Then she created a donation account where her readers could donate money to help pay for the books we needed.

Within less than a week, all of the money we needed was raised. I was shocked. This was the first time I had ever reached out to anyone online, and seeing her outpouring of support for someone she had never met blew my mind. A few weeks later, we received a copy of the book for every student. It was a magical moment, passing them out and explaining to the kids how we were able to secure a copy for each of them. But even better was watching the excitement and wonder on their faces as they read through the book and began deciding on which *Wreck This Journal* challenge they would complete first! The kids carried the books around with them everywhere, talking about them almost nonstop. It was truly something to behold.

I'd love to say that everything from that moment continued to get better. But as you know, sometimes when we step outside the box and do something different, not everyone views it as a win. The students had the books in their possession for about a week when I was called into a meeting with my principal. Another employee on our campus had come across the book we gave out. She was disgusted that we would give our kids a book that asked them to "destroy" the book in creative ways. She expressed her concern to the principal that all our students were going to begin destroying all books on campus and lose all respect for written text.

This employee was so upset she went to the central office as well. I was questioned about why I would buy a book like this and why it was purchased without approval. I was floored and tried explaining my thought process to those in charge. I tried to make them understand the kids loved the book and how we were using it to inspire creativity and whimsy.

In the end, the district decided I couldn't let the students keep the books at school. I had to send an apology letter to the parents of every fourth grader for giving them a book that I had secured without district approval. I also had to get their signature confirming they had received the letter.

The whole ordeal almost broke my spirit. I was embarrassed and upset. But something amazing still came of it. Twenty-seven parents wrote letters explaining the impact the book had already had on their children and how they would be going to speak to "the people in charge." It was a moving moment to see. And guess how many books were returned to us to destroy or keep away from kids? Not a single one.

A STORY FROM KEVIN BRADFORD
Special Education Teacher

In July 2016, one of the greatest apps of all time was released: Pokémon GO. My initial fascination with the game was due mainly to the fact that my sons were playing it, and it gave us a chance to spend time together before they went back to college. It gave us some great moments reminiscing about a game that we had played together on Game Boys when they were young.

As the beginning of school approached and I started to think about our theme, "Let the Adventure Begin," I wondered if I could incorporate Pokémon GO into my classroom. The more I played and thought about the app, I realized how much math there is in the game. Thus, the whole concept of "Let the Adventure Begin with Pokémon GO and Pokémon Math" emerged.

Fortunately, I work with a group of administrators who encourage teachers to take risks in the classroom. I started making plans to use the Pokémon GO app and the data in my math lessons. One drawback was our district firewalls and filters, which did not allow the game to work when connected. After pitching my idea to my principal and then to our district technology department, I was given permission to move ahead and the block was removed.

As a special education teacher, I work primarily with students who have learning differences, often significant. One of the most difficult things to do with these students is to keep them motivated when a task seems too difficult. Math is one of those tasks. But when I introduced Pokémon GO and Pokémon Math to my students, it was much easier than usual to motivate them to keep trying.

We used the combat points from the Pokémon that they caught to compare and order numbers. We used the distance that the students walked to teach decimals, and they had to chart how far they walked on a number line that we displayed in the hallway. The cost of things listed in the Pokémon GO store helped them learn about money and financial literacy. The height and weight of the Pokémon taught them about measurements. We used the egg hatching component to explore perimeter, area, and volume. The information in the game allowed me to teach my students many different lessons.

Overall, the purpose of using this app was to increase student success. I absolutely believe that was accomplished. If you look at how my students did on the state assessment, every student that participated in my math class for the whole year increased their score from the previous year, more than half of them by a significant amount. Even more important than that score is that every student walked away from my class that year with less anxiety about math and a better understanding that math can be found just about everywhere you look.

When you try to be different, it isn't always met with a smile and cheer. It doesn't always work perfectly in your first attempt. Sometimes you will be ridiculed. Sometimes you will be ostracized. Sometimes you will flat out be told, "No!"

If there is one thing I've taken away from the many times I've been given that alien look, it's that you can't give up. You can't ever stop trying do things better for kids. They deserve teachers who aren't afraid to step outside of their comfort zones and do something no one else is doing. Sometimes it will yield great results, and other times, it will be an epic fail. But it's worth the risk because sometimes that one small effort to innovate, or be a little more creative, makes a world of difference to a single student.

A STORY FROM DR. RONNIE (AND MYRA) GONZALEZ

Assistant Superintendent

As one of the assistant superintendents at Navasota ISD, I've had a little different view of Webb Elementary, especially since my daughter attends. Every mom and dad knows that when their child is in first grade, they need to have a special relationship with the tooth fairy. This year our daughter has lost four teeth, and all were lost at school. What's magical is that her teacher understands how important it is for kids to provide proof to the tooth fairy of the lost tooth.

When our daughter dropped her lost tooth in the cafeteria one day and could not find it, her teacher—quick thinker that she is—wrote a note to the tooth fairy explaining what happened and vouching that it was a lovely tooth. She even had the assistant principal co-sign the note to make it official.

Our daughter was so excited to be able to leave something special under her pillow and collect her money from the tooth fairy. It was a touching moment for us as parents, but it was also a reminder of how some teachers just go above and beyond to show how much they care.

Being different isn't easy. It's scary. It's challenging. It's a road filled with many potholes and speedbumps. But when you find that success, oh, it's all the more sweet. Don't ever stop trying to be different.

THINGS TO CONSIDER

- Have you tried to be different?
- What is standing in the way of you taking your creativity to the next level? How can you work around those obstacles?

Tweet your answers and tell your story at #KidsDeserveIt

CHAPTER 19

ASK ME

The closer we get to spring, it seems like the shorter our fuses get and the more rambunctious our students become.

As a classroom teacher, I always loved having those kids—the ones who come with warnings from their previous teachers, the ones who pushed every single button you had and a few you didn't know about, the ones who scream, curse, run, and say they hate you. Those are my kids. Those are the kids I'm drawn to.

We've all had those kids in our classes, and it's not easy. When we interact with these particular students, it's easy to let our emotions overtake us. Time and time again, I watch teachers get upset with a child over a choice the child made. I've seen teachers yell, call the student a liar or a loser, send the kid out into the hall, make the kid walk laps at recess, or sit at lunch detention. They try just about everything to make their point—except actually talking with the child.

A STORY FROM GERALYN JACKSON

School Counselor

The opportunity to counsel at John C. Webb Elementary has been so amazing that it is difficult to put into words. Every single person I'm surrounded with motivates me to aim higher and want better. Many people view the job of a school counselor as easy or less stressful simply because you are no longer in the classroom. It is not always easy, and it is often not even a sit-down job. It is usually at car rider pick up, lunch duty, and while walking in the hallways among the students that you tend to find out the struggles and social issues your students are facing. To counsel correctly, you need to have your fingertips on the pulse of the staff and student body. Relationships are key because if anyone on your campus, student or adult, is struggling physically or emotionally, then there is no way they are performing at their peak academically. As a team, we rise and we fall together.

As I sat in my office this past spring semester, I turned to find a familiar face standing quietly at my door. She said nothing and had been in a million times before. In fact, she and two of her friends were often verbally reprimanded for coming to the counselor's office way too often without a pass, and sometimes even without requesting permission, to talk about random, uneventful things. She was and still is the type of child the cover of back-to-school magazines always feature: skinny, well-dressed, perfectly tanned with long hair parted straight down the middle and a tiny pair of wire-framed glasses that let everyone who enters the room know that she's the one to sit by.

Her parents were still married and brought her to school every single day. Her grades were top-notch. As I stood and spoke to her, I extended my hand, and she took it. I was about to give my do-you-have-a-pass-or-does-your-teacher-know-you're-here-speech but abruptly chose not to because I realized she was alone. For the first time, she wasn't with her other over-achieving friends and likely was not just trying to dodge a simple assignment.

"Have a seat," I said, while posting a do-not-disturb sign on the door. "Is everything okay?"

"I just wanted to come see you," she replied.

"What's wrong?"

With that, she melted down into my arms for what seemed like an eternity. I assured her I was right there and even if I couldn't change her situation, I would listen and not judge her or tell her friends. I asked her to wait, and I called her teacher to say she was with me in my office, and I didn't know when she would be back to class, if at all. When she had finally composed herself, she told me some things she just wanted to get off her chest. My heart broke into a million pieces as she began to reveal her less-than-perfect home life, thoughts of suicide, and fears as to what the future held for her. I sat in awe as someone who seemed to have it all together and be on top of the world reminded me how important it is never to simply dismiss anyone. As I reflected on the time I had known her, both this year and last, I quickly realized all the small, mundane talk she had done in the past might have been because she had been building up the courage to share her true inner struggles. I had built the relationship with her, and I was grateful for it for multiple reasons. Looks can definitely be deceiving.

It was my high school students just a few years ago who once asked me, "Miss, why aren't you a counselor?" "Yeah, miss," several of them chimed in. "We would listen to you!"

What I realize now is that I do not take pride so much in them listening to me. More than anything, I want to always listen to them.

Educators work with kids who don't know how to control their emotions. We spend our days with kids who are taught at home to scream back at someone when they're upset with them, to shut down when someone is yelling at them so they can hide from the anger, and to use their fists instead of their words. Sure, we teach them otherwise at school. We teach them school expectations. But they're children. Those lessons are never one-and-done or even twenty-and-done. They are lessons we must teach again and again.

I see quite a few children in my office. Sometimes my emotions get the better of me, but I make every effort to sit with them, speak in a calm and quiet voice, and ask them what happened. I ask them to tell me their stories.

And do you know what some of them said?

"This morning my mom told me I was her stupid child. It made me so upset that all day I've been angry at everyone and can't figure out how not to be angry."

"The other boy said something about my dad. My dad is in the hospital, and I haven't seen him in three days, so when he said that, all I could see was red."

"Yes, I made a bad decision, but when my teacher saw, she screamed at me and told me she was sick of my behavior and brought me up here. She didn't even give me a chance to tell her I was sorry and that I knew better and wasn't thinking."

"I didn't get any sleep last night. We had our electricity turned off again and I had to take a cold shower at our neighbor's house. I was upset and let my emotions get the best of me."

And those are just the tip of the iceberg. Will kids frustrate us? Yes! Will they lie, manipulate, get angry, and disappoint us? Heck, yes!

So what can we do? We only have one choice. We have to be the adult, and that means putting away our own emotions, taking a breath, and having a conversation with the child in front of us. Not every poor choice a child makes has to have a consequence. Many times, you can talk to a child, clearly see they understand where they went wrong, and then move on with the day. We don't always make the right call. Many times, I find myself having to apologize to a child—or an adult, for that matter—for not handling a situation correctly. But that simple act of saying, "I'm sorry," can have a profound impact on another person.

And jumping straight into consequences doesn't always yield the result we're looking for. Come on, look at the kids who have lunch detention and who are walking laps at recess. If it's always the same kids, that punishment clearly isn't working.

Will having a conversation with a child always fix the problem? No. But it's our job as educators to grow every part of a child. And getting angry and sending them straight to the office before you take time to calmly talk to them destroys any relationship you're trying to build. That child simply comes to understand that you aren't in charge—the office is.

Let's take time this week to stop and talk with our students about their behavior.

A STORY FROM MELISSA BOENKER
Former Assistant Principal

Everyone talks about a person who has changed their lives. Sometimes that person is a parent, teacher, famous writer, speaker, or even an athlete. I had the pleasure of meeting my special person during my time serving at Webb Elementary as an assistant principal. This special person opened a window to a world I never understood or could even begin to understand.

Let me tell you a little about myself. I grew up on a farm in Waller, Texas, with a rice-farming father and a stay-at-home mom who became a very successful insurance agent. They worked hard to make a happy home for me and my two siblings. They knew some hard times, but they always seemed to provide more than enough of what we needed and wanted. We were expected to keep our grades high, complete chores, and stay active in our schools and communities. If you look back at our family albums, you would find us taking trips together, showing livestock, and celebrating birthdays and holidays with our relatives. I guess you could say we were a little spoiled. I certainly never really knew what it was like to live without something.

I entered the education field sixteen years ago. Along the way, I had the pleasure of teaching children of many different ages and with many different gifts and disorders. When I arrived at Webb, I felt very confident in my ability to work with all children—no matter their background. Then I met her.

My life changed forever that day in August 2016. She was a tough young lady. I had wanted to know the children who struggled with behaviors. Stories were shared about several children. I pulled data on referrals, and one child immediately raised a red flag. I think this child was in the office every couple of weeks. Her test scores were low, but teachers said she had potential. She was very smart, but her grades did not reflect her intelligence. School started and usually children don't seem to visit the office at the beginning of the school year, right? Soon enough, I met her. She would usually be sitting outside of the classroom, refusing to go in. She wore jeans and the same sweater with a hoodie every day. You could tell it was going to be a rough day when the hoodie was up as she got off the bus.

I liked to work the bus ramp in the mornings because you could get a beat on behaviors to come when the kids walked off the bus. Her bus came from an area in town that experiences high violence and drug abuse. People would tell me they were afraid to drive into that part of town alone. Many times, the children would get off the bus pushing and screaming at one another. I would try and defuse the situations and separate them if necessary. It was often the toughest part of my day. When this little girl would get off the bus with her hoodie up, I would say to myself, "Trouble is a comin', Boenker." I wouldn't shy away from her. I would attempt conversation and often received eye rolls, ewww-get-away looks, or the ever-famous "leave me alone" in response. Did I let that stop me? No. I guess you can call me persistent.

I would follow her to breakfast, trying to strike up a conversation, but many times, I was unsuccessful because she would end up in the office for disrespectful comments, leaving the class without permission, or refusing to work. Usually girls like to talk, right? Not this one. Her vocabulary had not improved much, and for weeks, her replies amounted to, "Leave me alone," "I ain't talking to you," or "I don't care."

During the one-sided conversations, I would explain what she should have done and lay out the consequence. I quickly figured out the consequence she absolutely hated was having to walk laps during recess or staying for after school detention. Disclaimer: If you know me well, you know I am a believer that positive behavior reinforcement is the only way to change behaviors but that some behaviors result in consequences.

At the beginning of the year, it would take me thirty minutes to an hour to get this student to walk her laps. She would refuse to budge, but I waited her out. I would sit next to her on the steps outside of the school—one of her many stopping points on the way to walk laps— and talk to her about how much it hurt me to punish her. I would talk to her even though she pretended not to listen, sometimes with her fingers in her ears, about changing her behaviors. I talked about all the teachers who cared about her, all the positive rewards that awaited her good behaviors, and how much I desperately wanted her to change because I knew she could have a different life if she wanted it. After about twenty minutes, I would tell her the laps would turn into after school detention if she didn't get up and walk. Many times, I would walk with her so she would know I was in this with her.

I would think about her often during the day, even when she wasn't in my office, which was a lot at the beginning of the year. I gathered information on her from teachers, counselors, and administrators. I read my behavior books, searching for ways to help her, and finally found a glimmer of hope from *Teacher's Encyclopedia of Behavior Management, 2nd Edition: 100+ Problems/500+ Plans* by Randy Sprick with Safe and Civil Schools. She needed to feel love from someone she didn't find threatening. She needed to feel needed. She needed responsibility. It occurred to me all of the things she needed were things I had growing up.

In time, one of our pre-kindergarten teachers, Mrs. Brooks, hired her to read to her children before nap time. After reading to them, she could go to recess with the rest of her class. She was shy at first and wasn't thrilled with the idea, but she didn't refuse to go. That was a first. There were even times when her teachers would call after recess to ask where she was, and I would find her napping next to the little ones. Who knows if she rested well at home or not, but she must have needed the rest. She needed those children, and they needed her. When they would see her in the hallway, they would yell hello or run up to hug her. I started to see her soften and even crack a smile. My window was opening. Time to open it a little further.

Her office visits started decreasing, but there were still times she would be sent to the office. I was thankful for those visits to the office. It gave us a chance to talk. Sometimes when it was too hard for her to talk, she would write. She had experienced pain in her lifetime. I could see it in her eyes. She would start to talk about something and then stop and say, "You just wouldn't understand." Finally, one day I told her, "You know, you're right. I don't understand. I didn't grow up like you did. I didn't have the painful experiences that you have had at such an early age, but that doesn't mean I don't care." There were times when she would talk a little, sharing her dream to become a volleyball player. We talked about the possibilities that would await her in junior high in the coming year and how she would get to participate in sports. I made her a poster for her binder of the Texas A&M volleyball team— 'cause I'm an Aggie—to remind her of the discussion we had about chasing her dreams. She even shared with me that one day she was going to deliver babies and aspired to be a nurse. She had finally started dreaming! Her pathway toward success was becoming visible.

She was also becoming part of my life. I would go home and share stories about her successes and failures with my family. My children started asking about her when I would come home from work. "Mom, how did she do today? Did she have to come to the office today?" Sometimes I wished I could bring her home with me. I did what I could. A colleague and I took her and her sister out for dinner one afternoon. It was amazing to watch her soak in everything around her. She looked at the guacamole on her plate and said, "What in the world is that? I'm not eating that!" That night she did not eat much, and I wondered if she liked the food, but she made sure to take the leftovers home. I wonder if that was her plan all along—eat a little and share the rest with her family. On her birthday, I bought her a birthday cake with candles and gave her a book she spotted at our recent book fair. She was beaming when she walked into her house with the cake to share with her family.

There was a time that I felt like my work was hopeless. It was right before Christmas break. She was acting out every day and starting to backtrack. I was questioning all of my work with her. Had I failed her? Todd had a tough conversation with her on a day that I wasn't there about loving people as much as they love you. I think that conversation opened her window even more. She wrote me a thank you card that I still carry around today in my purse, thanking me for everything I do for her and that she appreciated it even though she may not say it. That was the greatest Christmas present I could have ever hoped for. She did appreciate me.

After that, our conversations were more productive. Yes, she still struggled a little until the end of the year, but the number of referrals she had drastically decreased. The child who had scribbled on her state exam last year because she did not want to take it passed all three tests this year. She even chose to enroll in one advanced placement class in junior high because she believed she could do it.

I will never forget this one day, as she and I were walking and talking through a situation, she stopped me and looked me straight in the eye and said, "Are you going to be here next year?" That ripped my heart out. People were in and out of her life, and she just wanted to know if I'd do the same to her. Not knowing that I would be leaving Webb at the time, I asked her, "Well, are you going to be here? You are going to sixth grade, right?" She giggled a little. Then I told her we never know when a door might close and a window might open. That life is not predictable, but we should follow our hearts. I actually left Webb in March 2017 because I was offered a principal's position at another local elementary school in Navasota. It was an answer to my dreams but also the most difficult thing I've had to do in a long time. I had to leave a campus that had opened its heart to me and a little girl who had opened her heart to me. The day I had to announce to the staff that I was leaving, I made sure she could stay after school. When I called her mom, I made sure she understood she was not serving an after school detention, but that I needed to tell her something very important. I shed so many tears that day. We both cried when I told her the news, but I made sure I explained that my window was opening now and I needed to fly through it. I wanted her to know I was not leaving her. I would still be reachable and would visit her. She needed to see me chase my dreams just like I told her to chase hers.

I'm a believer that God places people in our lives for a reason. He placed her in my life to help me remember that I was placed on this earth to serve children and make a difference in their lives. I am forever thankful for her! I am forever thankful to Todd for giving me a chance to start my administrative career at Webb. Webb changed my life, and she changed my life forever.

THINGS TO CONSIDER

- Think about that one challenging student you got to know on a deeper level. How did you finally break through his or her walls? What helped? What didn't help?
- How can we continue to reach those kids who push us away?

Tweet your answers and tell your story at #KidsDeserveIt

CHAPTER 20

SEVEN SECONDS

It only takes a few seconds to make a judgment about someone or something. When someone new walks through our front doors for the first time, I figure I have less than seven seconds to leave them with a good first impression.

And in thinking about that, we've put a lot of time and effort into our front entryway—from adding more seating and a TV that displays tweets throughout the day, to computers for visitors to use, to building a log cabin to add to the school's aesthetic appeal. We even took our front desk greeter and placed her out in the foyer to better greet families as they arrive. And it has made a world of difference.

One of my favorite things that we've done is take photos of students throughout the year—playing at recess, eating lunch, learning in the classroom—and blow them up to 30' x 40' and print them on canvas. We then hang those giant canvas prints around the school. It's a powerful moment to walk the hallways of a school and see photos of smiling children who actually attend the school, learning and collaborating.

Because we were an academically underperforming school—according to the state's evaluation based solely on test scores—when I was brought in, we were assigned a Professional Service Provider (PSP) by the state of Texas. We worked with two women, Becky Harrison and Dr. Delic Loyde. These women are exceptional leaders and game changers. They challenged us, helped us grow, and continually encouraged us to strive to be better. Neither of those women were from Webb or Navasota. That's why, when writing this book, I thought it would be a great idea to ask Dr. Loyde, our most recent PSP, to share her reaction to walking into our school for the first time.

A STORY FROM DR. DELIC LOYDE

The first day I arrived at Webb Elementary, I knew it would be an adventure. Passing the neighborhood in the town with a view to the very end of the block, Webb Elementary looked on the outside to be just like any other elementary school. Regular brick with a circular drive, parents dropping off kids, and unloading buses all seemed pretty regular. But that is where the similarities ended.

The very entrance to the school was crafted into a facsimile of a fort that welcomed everyone who entered. I pondered if this entrance was just for the kids but quickly found out it was built for everyone—what a surprise! I chuckled a little and entered "Fort Webb." I began to look around and was taken aback by the high energy of the campus. Students and staff were interacting positively. Laughter was in the air. You could feel the positivity in the air. The walls were colorful and displays showed student work as well as student and staff affirmations.

An administrator was sitting on the floor quietly, speaking with a student who seemed to be having a bad day. A secretary was helping a parent find the cafeteria. So far, so normal. As I walked to classrooms, a student opened a door for me and introduced me to his class. I observed the class for a while as the teacher continued with instruction, and the students remained engaged in their learning. As I journeyed to the next classroom, I was intrigued by a note from a teacher on her door that said, "Please come see me teach!" Now that's different. During my visit, I realized this message was on every classroom door every day, indicating what the teacher was teaching and inviting visitors to observe. This was not for a scheduled observation or teacher evaluation—it was part of the culture of the school. Students and teachers were eager for others to see teaching and learning in all of its messiness on a daily basis at this school. Any time, any day, no appointment needed—how powerful!

I spent several hours going from classroom to classroom accepting the invitation to see teaching and learning. I thought, *What a cool concept!* Yes, indeed. This is a cool school. This is what a school should look like. This is what a school should feel like. This is what a school should smell like. Not just a building. Not just a place where people work or a place where parents just drop off their children, but a real school—a place where children can feel love, take risks, make mistakes, dust themselves off, and learn more than even they could imagine was possible. A place where students and teachers can become their best selves.

My role at Webb Elementary includes building capacity for improving student outcomes. My needs assessment of a school begins by looking at the systems within the school that are already providing the most positive impact on student outcomes. These systems are the strengths of a school. At Webb Elementary, the primary system that supports the success of students within the school can be found in the name of the school itself.

THE WEB AT WEBB

Webb is a very appropriate name for this school because Webb Elementary is a school based on relationships—a virtual web of relationships. It is evident even before you walk through the doors of the school that students, teachers, parents, and community members are all interconnected and that everyone strives to renew their commitment on a daily basis to the philosophy that "Kids Deserve It." Webb Elementary is composed of an intricate web of relationships that support and exist for each one to teach all students that:

- School is a place of daily wonder and excitement.
- School is a place where kids can be themselves.
- School is a place where you feel safe.
- School is a place where learning is a social activity and progress is expected.

WONDER AND EXCITEMENT

What makes school interesting? Why should kids want to come to school each day? Students are eager to find their "Wow!" at this school. Webb Elementary is a school that certainly provides that "Wow!" factor for kids. It is a school where you can be a rock star and a superhero all in the same week. Students are able to take a virtual field trip to the North Pole and actually feel the chill. Students can find their "Wow!" every day. They know that their school is a place where they can make a dinosaur, a mobile, a race car, or whatever they envision. Their school has its own makerspace, so anything is possible!

FREE TO BE ME

The best learning occurs when and where students are free to be themselves. Students are encouraged to develop resilience and a positive image of themselves at this school. Webb Elementary is a school where students are told how special they are every day. Celebrations occur daily. Teachers know students on such a deep level that students feel safe to reveal their hidden talents. Teachers respond by helping students develop in every area possible.

SAFETY

Safety is a top priority for any school. Webb elementary is a school that is internally composed of "houses" to give students and staff a sense of community. Visitors are welcome every day. Parents, grandparents, friends, and community are invited on special days to engage with students. Students create and participate in activities inside and outside of the school that build community. Teachers make an extra effort daily to help students develop a sense of belonging at the school. The school provides a safety net for the many students who come from impoverished backgrounds.

LEARNING EVERY DAY

Webb Elementary is a school where the principal comes to your class regularly to read and tells you about his favorite books on the daily announcements. This is a school where you can identify a community problem as an elementary student and create your own community service project to solve the problem.

This school allows students to be the teacher in front of everyone while the teacher is a student trying to learn from them. At Webb, students can be "sentence doctors" and "paragraph surgeons." This school is so cool that even the mayor drops by to read. Students share their writing publicly and have a writing wall. The school hosts Family Reading Nights. Literacy is important here!

Now that I am in my second year at Webb Elementary, I can still say the same thing about the school that I thought on that very first day—this is a cool school! The student outcomes show it! Webb Elementary has met standard with an incredibly challenged student population. It is an honor to continue to support the transformation of this campus. The key to Webb's success lies in the relentless campus commitment to creating an atmosphere for learning that truly meets the needs of students, even if that means that the staff need to learn new strategies along the way.

How many other schools would take the risk to make this depth of commitment to improve student outcomes? How many school leaders are dedicated enough to be the change that is necessary to inspire improvement and strive for excellence? How many school leaders and teachers are selfless enough to support a school environment of perpetual energy to meet the needs of their students? Still looking? Webb elementary is the archetype that others can learn from. This school is a place that dares to give kids what they truly deserve—our very best every single day.

———————

At Webb Elementary, we don't claim to be perfect. We don't claim to have everything figured out. What we do promise to do is make decisions that are in the best interest of our children. To make sure the decisions we make are decisions that are what's best for kids, and not what's easiest for adults. Like other schools all around the world, we hope all who enter our walls will leave with that feeling that something special is happening here.

THINGS TO CONSIDER

- How do you set a good first impression in your classroom or school?
- How can your students play more of a role in shining the light on your school's greatness?

Tweet your answers and tell your story at #KidsDeserveIt

CHAPTER 21

DO YOU KNOW MY NAME?

Throughout *Kids Deserve It!*, we talked about the importance of building relationships. Not only building relationships with students, but also parents and colleagues. Those strong relationships are the foundation for everything we do in our classrooms.

A STORY FROM JESSICA MCHALE

Second Grade Teacher

Ever since I can remember, I wanted to be a teacher. I wanted to make a difference in students' lives. When I was in school, I hated being told to think a certain way and that I had to conform to a little box. I also disliked that my teachers really knew nothing about me. Therefore, when I became a teacher I vowed to be different. I wanted to be more energetic, more engaging, and more connected to my students.

In 2012, my dream finally became reality. I graduated from SHSU with a teaching degree, and in 2013, I became a junior high theatre arts teacher. As much as I loved it, that wasn't my true calling, so the following year I became an elementary school teacher. That's where I found my passion and babies who needed me. I take every group of kids each year and make sure I know them as well as I can to build strong relationships with them and their parents. Teacher-student relationships are one of the most important things to successful students, in my opinion. If you don't care about those children or know anything about them, how can you help them reach their full potential?

You might be thinking you have no idea where to start to build these relationships. Here are just a few of the things I do that seem to make a world of difference. First, I handwrite a welcome letter to every single student on my roster before school starts. Our principal had mentioned this a few years ago, and while some teachers duplicate letters, I write each student an individual note to tell them how excited I am that they're going to be in my class and that I can't wait for us to meet. At Meet the Teacher night, I have a little gift waiting for them, along with a newsletter that has pictures and information about me. My students love this! Because I do this, my students are already somewhat comfortable with me on day one. On the first day of school, we play a name game so that by the end of the first day, I have *all* of my students' names memorized. You might not think this is a big deal, but it means the world to these kids that you call them by name on the second day of school. It makes them a somebody. I also give them a short questionnaire to fill out, so I learn a little more about them. In my classroom, we spend the first three days of school getting to know one another with games and activities.

By the end of the week, we all know one another pretty well.

To keep this going throughout the year, I still have a few other tricks up my sleeve:

1. I don't make them do anything I wouldn't do when it comes to work or presentations.
2. We do "GoNoodle" together. Yes, I dance and act goofy with my kids. Again, this goes back to my first rule.
3. I color with them. If we're doing some kind of project or activity that involves coloring, I get on the floor and do it with them.
4. Flexible seating that gets moved. I have stools, balls and bean bags in my room. Everyone gets a turn as long as you can handle it. Misbehave, and you lose the privilege.
5. Weekly treasure box. For every above-and-beyond good deed you do, your name goes on a ticket in my reward jar. At the end of the week, I pull some names. If your name gets pulled, you get a trip to the treasure box. And guess what? It's an actual treasure box!
6. Go outside for lessons. Who says you always have to teach inside at a desk or table? Take it outside, shake it up a bit.
7. Play music in class. I have always been a huge music lover, so why change that just because I teach? Every day my students come into my class to music. We work to music and read and paint to music.
8. Assign class jobs with real responsibility—even to those students who are challenging. I give them responsibility and something to be proud of.
9. Talk to them, not at them, above them, or down to them. Kids know when you're being real and when you're faking it.
10. Genuinely care about their feelings and what they're

going through. If you don't, they'll figure it out, anyway. Above all things, these babies just want love and honesty. They don't always get everything they need at home, so it's up to us to make sure they get it somewhere safe.

I have found that we're not just teachers. We're mothers, fathers, nurses, counselors, listeners, and fixers of all things. Our students look up to us to teach and guide them, and in return, we get their love and smiles! And that, my friends, is the greatest gift of all.

One thing I've seen that makes an enormous impact when teaching children is simply knowing someone's name. My first name is Todd. It's easy to pronounce. My last name, Nesloney, is another story. I can't even tell you how many times I've had to correct someone on the pronunciation of my last name. When people would mispronounce it the first time, it never bothered me. But I clearly remember being annoyed when a central office administrator in my former district, who had worked with me for many years, regularly mispronounced my name. It bothered me. This person who had known me for years still couldn't say my name correctly.

As a teacher, and now an administrator, I make it a point to pronounce names correctly. And I also talk with teachers when they have students in their own classrooms whose names they are still saying incorrectly because "it's difficult."

During my first year as principal at Webb, I was working hard to learn the names of all the staff members. There was one staff member I had talked with several times, and one day, she dropped by my office to ask if she could speak with me briefly. As we sat down, she told me that she had worked in Navasota for many years, and never, not once, had any of her former administrators pronounced her name correctly. She said it bothered her, but added, "After you correct them so many times and they don't change, what's the point?" I loved that she sat me down to tell me how much it meant to her, and from that day on, I pronounced her name correctly and corrected others when they said it wrong.

Our names hold much value. For some people, their names are all that they have. It's all that they can control in their environment. As educators and as good citizens, we owe it to people to not only learn their names but also learn how to pronounce them correctly. It can make all the difference.

THINGS TO CONSIDER

- What can you do to make every child feel special and appreciated in your classroom and school?
- Have you taken the time to learn the names of students who aren't in your classroom?

Tweet your answers and tell your story at #KidsDeserveIt

CHAPTER 22

SAFE

We all want to create a school environment where students and staff feel safe. We work tirelessly to ensure not only our students' physical safety in a school environment but also their emotional safety.

A STORY FROM JESSICA SCHUTZENHOFER
Second Grade Teacher

It was the end of the first nine weeks of school, and I was preparing to receive a transfer student from another class. I wasn't just his second teacher, but his third. This student was known for his temper and lack of effort. I was absolutely terrified and had no idea what to expect from this boy. Before he was moved into my classroom, I had a meeting with Mr. Marvel, our former assistant principal, to go over some guidelines. Some of these guidelines included keeping distance between the student and me, giving him breaks when he seemed overwhelmed, and having a plan in place if I needed to evacuate my class. Yes, it was definitely a little intimidating for a second-year teacher.

My next step was to tell my class that we would be getting a new student. They all knew him, and were aware of his previous actions. I told my class that this was his fresh start, everyone deserved one, and we were giving him his. We were also having a transition period to help this student adjust to my class procedures and expectations. This transition period was a great help to the student and to me.

Once in my class, the student was still behaving as he had in his previous classrooms. He wanted to sleep all day, draw, and just do whatever he wanted. That was not going to work for me. I told myself something had to be different. I just didn't know exactly where to begin. Like the other teachers, I took time to get to know this boy, but it still didn't feel like it was enough. I had to figure out some other way to reach him.

As the days went on, I spent a little more time each day just talking with this boy about his interests and his family. Come to find out, he loved the Marvel comic books. His love for the comics is what helped me truly make a connection with him. I would balance the time between learning and just hanging out with this student. If he had done so much work for me, he received so much free time throughout the day.

When he began to feel comfortable around me, he opened up even more. The stories he told were truly heartbreaking, and I started to understand why he would rather be at home with his family than in my class. I assured him that no matter what happened with his family, he would still have a teacher to turn to who loved him. We had some bumps in the road along the way, but we took it a day at a time. Throughout the remainder of the school year, we continued to learn from each other. It wasn't easy, but in the end, it was the most rewarding experience I'd had in my teaching career. I realized that a little love and a safe environment can change a student's outlook on everything. Eventually, instead of wanting to go home when he got in trouble, this student was more upset about not being in the classroom. This was huge progress. This boy, who had never wanted to be in school, now wanted to change his behavior to be able to stay in class. It was only my second year of teaching, but I learned what has been the biggest lesson of my career. I learned from this student that teaching is more than just teaching the skills students need to move on to the next grade. Teaching is about helping students feel the love you have for them. For some, it might be the only love they know. This experience taught me the importance of each individual connection and building an environment where every child feels valued. This student will always hold a special place in my heart, and I love to hear about all he has accomplished since leaving my classroom.

There are many **things we can't control** as educators. We can't ensure that our students get a good night's sleep the night before. We can't guarantee they are well-fed and bathed when they go home at night. We can't make certain our students are told how wonderful they are or how brilliant they are when they get home. So much of their lives are out of our control, and it's probably one of the more difficult aspects of being a teacher. It's difficult because your students become your children, and that's a bond many people in other fields don't always understand. You ache for them, lose sleep over them, even spend hundreds, if not thousands, of your own dollars on them. When you spend almost seven hours every day with a child, it's hard not to become attached.

As a campus leader, I see the struggles our children face on a much larger scale. I deal with many more CPS calls, home visits, and parent meetings than I ever did as a teacher. That was one of the biggest eye openers for me in my transition from teaching to campus administration. I wasn't expecting the constant barrage of safety concerns that included everything from campus security, custody disputes, and issues of physical, emotional, and sexual abuse. When I was a teacher, I never realized the hours administrators spend just consoling students and their family members. I never realized how long it can take to calm down a child on the verge of a breakdown.

And why hadn't I seen that as a teacher? Because as the principal, sometimes it's your job to bear the load. A principal deals with many dark issues that cannot be discussed with the entire staff. Sometimes I can pull aside the teachers who have those students and fill them in on what's happening, but sometimes I can't. That reality makes it even more difficult when I miss a scheduled walk-through, or a class read-aloud, or a play-date at recess, and, due to privacy laws, I can't fully explain why I couldn't make it there on time. But that's how this job works.

Our students and parents are bringing so much baggage to school when they walk through those doors, and as we said in *Kids Deserve It!*, I truly believe our job as educators is to leave our mess in the car. We have to show up, ready to tackle whatever comes, ready to fill our classrooms and media centers and cafeterias with warmth and safety, because that is what our kids and families deserve.

A STORY FROM DARLA DAVIS

Third Grade Teacher

There was a day after Donald Trump became president that one of my students came to school very distraught. I knew something was wrong, so I started talking to him and, from those conversations, he conveyed through tears that he was sad and worried.

After further discussing what I could do to help him, he shared with me that his father was going to have to go back to his home country and leave the rest of the family because he didn't have his papers. My heart sank, and I felt the concern and sadness that he felt. He was concerned that our new president wanted to build a wall and send all undocumented immigrants back to their homeland.

That evening I struggled with the news this young, precious child had shared with me, and I was filled with sadness. I had to search for the words to comfort this little boy and somehow convey that everything was going to be all right, even though I wasn't sure. I felt as powerless as this child! I continued to have conversations with him to assure that he was safe and loved and that everything was going to work out okay.

That was such a powerful moment when I realized he had shared something so significant with me, and he knew I would always be there for him. I continue to pray for him and his family.

With the political world we now live in, there are many students—and entire families—facing fears some of us have never experienced in our lifetimes. In the area where Webb is located, there seems to be an overwhelming sense of uneasiness and fear regarding the future of some of our families.

In times like these, a school becomes more than just an educational institution. It becomes a safe place. A constant in someone's life. It becomes a place they can go to feel loved and protected. We never know the bags that others are carrying with them every day. Whether it's a child or co-worker, it's important for us to do all we can to create environments where others can thrive and excel.

A STORY FROM KVON LAMBERT
Second Grade Teacher

School. What is a school? The formal definition is an institution designed to provide learning spaces and learning environments for the education of students or pupils under the direction of teachers. Some students might say school is a place where they feel alone, ridiculed, and disliked. That is what school was like for me.

I am the oldest of four girls. My parents divorced when I was nine. My mom did not have a college degree, but she was a very hard worker. She began working any place she could to provide for us. She worked long hours at multiple jobs just about every day. The income from these jobs was barely enough for us to get by. I was the babysitter when school was over. My sisters were five, four, and three. Daycare for four kids would have been way too expensive. We tried at-home daycare, and it was a disaster.

I remember school during this time, and as a young African American girl, it was awful. I never did my homework. I rarely talked or participated in class. My fourth grade teachers were awful. They never asked why my homework wasn't done. One would scold me and send me to the teacher next door to talk some sense into me. The teacher next door would tell me how I would never amount to anything if I didn't start doing my work. They never talked to me about home or what was going on there. I was miserable, and I got into fights on a regular basis. I had one friend, and I managed to mess that up too. I felt like I couldn't do anything right, and I was in the slow learner group. I had a lot going on, and I did not feel like school was a safe place. School was a place where black people were always in my face, telling me what I should have done. It was a place where white people were telling me I was dumb. And they were all in agreement that I was bad. There was no discrimination—I just felt like all teachers disliked me!

Fifth grade was the turning point for me. We moved and I got a very old teacher. She was awesome. She could do this weird trick with her arms, and we all loved it. My very old teacher took interest in us. She talked to us, played with us, and encouraged us to do our best. I remember the day she came to me and told me, "You don't belong in this slow learner class. You are very capable of doing the work." She had me moved to a different class, and that teacher also gave me the you-can-do-it talk.

I decided to become a teacher to be like those two teachers. I am here to make sure my students have fun while they learn. I want my students to do their best. I want them to feel loved and know they are in a safe environment. I want my students to remember me as the teacher who gave them all those things.

During my second year of teaching, I was doing well with making sure I lived up to my own expectations until I got caught up in educating. I attempted to stop playing so much and tried to introduce more learning into the workday. We only had share time once a week. The closed fist for silence prevailed time and time again. We didn't have time to sing all those songs! I cut my morning STEM centers out and began doing only educational centers. Unwanted behaviors hit the ceiling, and I had lunch detentions left and right. I had no idea what was wrong! I was doing my best to get my students to the desired point. I evaluated my behavior sheets and thought about what I was doing differently. I realized I had cut out all the fun. I was no longer interacting with my students. I was so wrapped up in getting them all on a particular reading level that I had little time to make sure they were having fun. I was no longer concerned about talking to them about what they did over the weekend. "Voices off" was repeated too many times during the day. I stopped giving so many hugs and holding hands with them to make sure they felt loved. I had become the teacher who only cared about the product and not the person.

Relationships have to come first in education. I immediately went back to what was working. I want to be successful in educating my students, but I never want to forget that they are grown-ups in little bodies. They have feelings, and they need to be loved as well as educated. Creating good relationships with my students will always be my first priority. I feel that learning will come much easier if I apply love, attention, and trust first and most effectively.

School should be a place that provides a safe space, an institution designed to provide learning environments for the teaching of students under the direction of teachers, students, administrators, and staff. School should be a place where long-lasting positive relationships are created and duplicated throughout a lifetime.

Yes, our job is to educate the children who are sent to us. But as I've said time and time again, you can't reach a child's head until you reach their heart. We have to be creating these environments where children feel valued, celebrated, and, most of all, safe. We can't expect them to be brave in their learning and decisions if they're fearful of that failure and rejection.

THINGS TO CONSIDER

- When was the last time you took a few moments to sit and talk with a student or your administrator—just to see if they were okay?
- What are you doing to create the kind of environment where others feel safe?

Tweet your answers and tell your story at #KidsDeserveIt

CHAPTER 23

CONNECT WITH PARENTS TOO

We talk often about how important it is to build relationships with our students, but it is equally important to build quality relationships with their parents and guardians.

There are so many schools that start working on building relationships even before day one. Some teachers and administrators make home visits before the first day of school, as well as throughout the year. In *Kids Deserve It!*, I talked about the hot dog cookouts we host every semester. I also know teachers who will call home to five students a week just to tell their families how awesome their child is.

Another thing we do at our district office in Navasota is purchase a bunch of books for kids two weeks before school starts. Then on a Saturday, we will select addresses of about 100 families from our campus and, as a staff, we will go out and make home visits to introduce ourselves and drop off books. We tell them we can't wait for the year to start and invite them to Meet the Teacher night.

It is a great opportunity for us to have some face-to-face contact with the families but also an opportunity to provide them with at least one more book in their home. I loved the experience of driving across town to pass out the books and meet more families. My goal over the next two or three years is to make it a point to visit the homes of every single student on my campus. This year I'm starting with the homes of the third through fifth graders. It will be a challenge but one I know will be worth it.

A STORY FROM MELISSA NEUMANN
Fourth Grade Teacher

It is imperative, as a teacher, to form a connecting relationship with your students each year but also just as important to do the same with their parent or guardian. You have to establish a bond with parents, gaining their trust and the belief that together you are a team to help their children succeed.

Yes, there are parents you can never seem to reach. Keep calling or call a relative. They always pass on the message that "the teacher called." Make sure you tell them you are calling to "check in" or talk about something good that their child did. You'll also have the parent who just doesn't respond. Again, be persistent or even make a home visit.

I had a community member tell me she noticed during her early evening walks around the neighborhood that there are times when my car is the only one in the parking lot. I was making phone calls! Log your calls, record who you talked to, and make a note of what you discussed. You will be surprised at what a difference this makes.

I also always follow up the next day and tell the students how much I enjoyed visiting with their parents. Most parents do love and care about their children, even if it's not the way we, as educators, think it should be. We must respect that and understand these parents are doing the best they know how.

One afternoon as I drove home, I came to a stop sign and noticed an older woman with many heavy grocery sacks walking on the side of the street. I rolled down my window and said hello. She stopped and stared at me. I then proceeded to ask her if I could give her a ride. I never do this. I didn't even know why I was doing it right then, but I felt led to give her a ride, and I couldn't ignore that feeling within me.

Without any hesitation, she got in my car. We exchanged pleasantries as she directed me to her house. When she got out, she thanked me and asked, "Are you a teacher?" I said yes and told her my name and where I worked. We said our good-byes, and off she went.

The next morning, one of my students came up to me. He told me about his grandmother. It was the woman I had given a ride to the night before! What are the odds? He came to me, gave me a big hug, and told me I was the topic of conversation at the dinner table! He thanked me for picking up his grandmother and explained their car was not working, they'd needed groceries, and none of the neighbors would drive her.

I have never stopped and picked up a stranger before. Something told me to do it that day, and it was such a powerful moment. I was so **glad to be in the right place** at the right time.

Connecting with our students is important. When we take the time to truly connect with the parents and guardians in their life, we end up forging even deeper connections.

Maybe that means we make a home visit. Maybe we go to a student's after school event. Maybe we just make sure a parent gets a phone call from us every couple of weeks. Whatever it might be, building those relationships up with your students' families makes all the difference.

THINGS TO CONSIDER

- How do you connect with your students' families?
- How many student homes have you visited? How can you visit more? What is holding you back?

Tweet your answers and tell your story at #KidsDeserveIt

CHAPTER 24

LEADERS PARK IN THE BACK

There's something perplexing about principals that I've always seen depicted in television and movies. Truthfully, I see it at many schools I visit. I'm talking about that assigned parking spot at the front of the school marked "Principal."

I've never understood that. It never made sense to me why a leader of a school would get a designated parking spot. The cafeteria workers work hard for our kids. The campus secretary works hard for our kids. The instructional aides work hard for our kids. So why is there one person on campus who is glorified with the private parking spot?

I also have heard stories about a row of parking spots at the front of the school reserved for those who work in the front office. What kind of message are we sending to our students and our community with these special parking arrangements?

I knew that was going to be something I eliminated immediately. Why? Because in my mind, the administrators should park in the back. As a leader, everything we do sets an example for others. I want to be the kind of leader who leaves front parking spots for others.

It might seem insignificant to some. But for me, it has been a big deal. I am no better than any other adult or child who walks onto the school property. Why would I ever believe it's okay to put myself on such a pedestal?

Sometimes we have to sit at the table and let everyone else get their food first. Sometimes we have to hold the door and let twenty people walk through before we go inside. Sometimes we have to stay at the school and wait until every child leaves before we go home. And sometimes, as leaders, we need to park in the back. We need to stay humble, serve others, and you know what? A few extra steps to the school never hurt anyone!

THINGS TO CONSIDER

- What are you doing, even unintentionally, that could be seen as thinking you're better than others?
- In what new way can you put someone else first today?

Tweet your answers and tell your story at #KidsDeserveIt

CHAPTER 25

CLASSROOM CHAMPIONS

When I was still teaching fifth grade, I was passionate about connecting my students to the world. I wanted my students in this tiny Texas town to be able to learn from and alongside people from all walks of life.

We often had Skype calls or Google Hangouts sessions with authors, athletes, celebrities, community helpers, and other classrooms from all over the world. It was important to me to provide my students, many who would never leave the state of Texas, with a broader worldview. I wanted to show them how others lived and learned in other parts of the world and that they have many things in common with people from different cultures who live in different states and countries.

And let me tell you, it blows a fifth grader's mind when she finds out someone in Sweden knows who Katy Perry is. Or when a third grader in Australia knows what an Xbox 360 is. It helps them see that, despite what our politicians post on social media, we all have things in common. It helps them see we're not so different, and we can find a common ground and collaborate and work together.

One day we had scheduled a Skype call with a third grade class in Australia, and because of the time change, we had to make the call at 5:30 p.m. one evening. I had more than fifty of my seventy-five students show up! Do you know why? Two reasons. One was they wanted to hear the Australian accent. The other reason was my students had figured out that 5:30 p.m. on a Thursday evening in Texas was 8:30 a.m. on Friday morning in Australia. They would be Skyping with the future. They were so excited! It was a great call, and through it, we discovered those third graders were learning the exact same things we were learning in science.

Afterward I had an idea. We had really started using Google Drive tools, and I knew from talking with the Australian students' teacher, they had as well. So we decided to have our kiddos all do a project together. The Australian third graders partnered with my fifth graders, and together they selected a science topic, researched it, created a Google Slides presentation, and presented it via Skype. It was amazing! My fifth graders were beaming. And think about it—they were able to move on to the next grade bragging about doing a project with a student from Australia—one they had never met.

While perusing the "Skype in the Classroom" website looking for organizations and classrooms to connect my class with, I stumbled across an ad for Classroom Champions. This particular group allowed you to submit your name for the possibility of being selected to have a Google Hangout session with an Olympic athlete. Say what? I submitted our name right away, hoping with all my might we'd get selected. And we did!

Our Google Hangout was with Olympic Gold Medalist Steve Mesler, and it was fantastic. Steve effortlessly connected with my students and talked with them about their short-term and long-term goals. He showed us his gold medal, which he earned while on the U.S. men's bobsled team, and discussed the kinds of goals athletes must set to reach those high levels. It was one of those pinch-me experiences.

From that Google Hangout, I learned Steve had co-founded the Classroom Champions organization with his sister, Leigh Parise. They started it to get top-performing Olympic and Paralympic athletes to partner with classes to teach them skills like the aforementioned goal setting, teamwork, community building, and so much more. The athletes create videos and share them with teachers across the country. And anyone can get these videos for free on their website at classroomchampions.org.

After our Google Hangout, Steve told me how, every spring, they select teachers from Title 1 schools to be a Classroom Champions teacher. So of course I applied. Lo and behold, we were selected and paired with Paralympian Joshua Sweeney. Josh had fought in Afghanistan, stepped on an IED, and lost both of his legs. After that tragedy, he came back to the United States and joined the U.S. men's sled hockey team. That was the year he was our athlete.

Throughout the year, we received different video lessons from Josh. We also were able to connect with him in two Google Hangout sessions. It was a phenomenal experience. What made it all the more special was the year Josh was our athlete was also the year of the Winter Paralympics in Sochi, Russia. We were able to watch him train and then compete in Russia. He ended up scoring the winning goal that helped the U.S. team win the gold medal. It was thrilling.

But the most amazing part came when we entered ourselves into a video contest Classroom Champions was sponsoring. My students created a video telling Josh's life story. I was so proud of their ideas and the hard work they put into it. When our video was selected as the winner, Josh visited our school, spoke to our entire student population, and spent the morning sharing stories with my students.

It was a powerful moment. Josh shared his story, showed everyone his gold medal, and took questions from the students. One of my students asked him flat out, "Are you angry you don't have any legs?" A hush fell over the group, and I swear I heard a teacher or two gasp. Josh took a second, turned his head, and looked that young man straight in the face and said, "Not at all. You know, I could wake up every morning and be angry about what happened to me, and for a little while right after it happened, I was. But then I realized, instead of living in that anger, I could make the choice to live the best life I can with the life I've been given. Why be angry about something I can't change? And look at it this way, I wouldn't be a gold medalist had this all not happened to me." Wow. His words took my breath away. His visit was something my students talked about for months afterward.

I don't think Josh will ever fully understand the impact he had on my students, or on me, that day. The experience was so profound that I now make a point of mentioning Classroom Champions every time I have a speaking engagement or work with another school.

A STORY FROM CASSIE REYNOLDS
Fourth Grade Teacher

Three years ago, I was blessed to be a part of a once-in-a-lifetime opportunity. Our entire campus participated in the Classroom Champions program. As a Classroom Champions mentee, you are assigned an Olympian or Paralympian who sends videos throughout the year. You also get to video chat twice a year with them. The year we moved to Webb, a former fourth grade teacher and I continued the program, and this past year, I was the only teacher participating on our campus.

Every year I see tremendous growth in my students as part of the program. Through Classroom Champions, my students have learned to set goals, learned about the importance of integrity and community, as well as perseverance. As a teacher in my fourth year in the program now, I have seen firsthand the overwhelming positive impact that Classroom Champions has on our students. In the beginning of the year, I had several introverts and students who were hesitant to try new things. Through monthly lessons and activities, I have seen my students' confidence grow immensely. They are honest about their goals, setbacks, and are not afraid of making mistakes because they know it is a learning process.

One of my students had a very tough third grade year. He was reserved, had behavior problems, and his mother told me he did not like coming to school. Since he has been in the Classroom Champions program, I have seen him blossom. He is no longer shy, but is very outgoing and has many friends in fourth grade. When we met for parent conferences, his mother told me he now looks forward to coming to school.

He loves having the opportunity to partner with a Paralympian who takes the time to mentor our class on topics we need help with the most. His mother has also seen a major change at home; she said he acts more responsible as an older brother to his sister and around the house. I know that Classroom Champions has helped give him and others the tools necessary to overcome obstacles and become more confident individuals.

With the support of Classroom Champions, we have also helped organize a campus-wide food drive and provide necessities for others in our community. About 88 percent of our students fall below the poverty line, so when you see them show up to give even more to others, it's a moving experience. Programs like Classroom Champions have helped me organize my kids and teach them so many skills that will far outlast the day or year in my classroom. I appreciate the positive impact Classroom Champions has had not only on my students but also on myself as I've been involved. It has inspired all of us to be the best in all that we do. Sometimes it just takes a champion to give us that extra little nudge. I would recommend any and every teacher apply for this life-changing program.

We must take advantage of any opportunity we have to grow our students emotionally as well as academically—especially when it's free. Programs like Classroom Champions are a no-brainer to me because they use sports, something so many of our students love, to connect them to exceptional role models from all walks of life and experiences. Like I always say, our job as educators is 50 percent academic and 50 percent emotional. The moment we focus more on one than the other, we are no longer doing our job.

THINGS TO CONSIDER

- In what ways are you teaching your students character education skills?
- How can you connect your kids to people outside of their normal circles?

Tweet your answers and tell your story at #KidsDeserveIt

CHAPTER 26

PUSH ME

After teaching for a few years, you can find yourself becoming complacent or even jaded. There have been days in my career when I have wondered if teaching was really meant for me. Some days are dark. The pressure can be overwhelming, and sometimes you have to work with people who don't share your teaching philosophies.

On social media, I discovered there are scores of people who are ready to tear you down at a moment's notice. But I am not one to sit around and be idle or believe others' lies about myself. Instead, I have discovered the importance of surrounding myself with people who will push me and make me better. I have also worked to avoid creating an echo chamber of fellow educators who only tell me that I'm amazing.

Because of tools like Twitter, Facebook, Instagram, Periscope, and Voxer, I have been able to communicate daily with educators from all walks of life and experiences. These conversations have taught me more about other cultures and beliefs than I ever could have gained from reading a textbook.

When I connect with these other educators, a primary goal is to find someone who will challenge my thinking and help me grow. We all have those days when we doubt our gifts. We all sometimes feel like we're just going through the motions and can't break out of a rut. And we all have those days when we feel like all our colleagues are spewing nothing but negativity. It's difficult, especially when you're a person who maintains a positive outlook, and it can eat away at your soul no matter how strong you are.

That's when I turn to my support system for advice. It's important to surround yourself with people who can be honest with you and tell you when you're acting like an idiot or confirm when your fears are valid.

If you've been teaching for very long, you know there is constant risk of becoming complacent. We have to keep pushing ourselves to be better. Sometimes all it takes is finding that one person who will walk alongside us, kicking our butt into gear when we need it.

A STORY FROM SUE AMBRUS

Head Start Liaison

All I ever wanted to do was teach, but when I first went to college, right out of high school, my parents said I had to do something else because "there is no money in teaching." My first attempt at college did not go so well. I went into teaching after many years of working as an administrative assistant for various companies. With my degree in hand, I was ready to tackle the world of early childhood education.

I love teaching, and my first few years were wonderful. I would transform my room into an underwater fantasy world or a trip to outer space. Somewhere along the way, I lost that sense of wonder and excitement. I got worn down by "those" kids, "those" parents, and "those" tests, but mostly by negative people who surrounded me constantly.

One day a new teacher came to kindergarten. She was much younger than I was, but we hit it off right away. Her enthusiasm and sparkle helped me remember that there is "magic" for children and that I can make that happen. So now I make sure to remember the magic. My students are amazed at some of the things that happen in our classrooms. Things that seem simple to me are magical to them. The act of mixing two colors in front of them and getting a third color while reading *Mouse Paint* or the way their faces light up when our friend Pete the Cat shows up make the fantasy real for all of us.

My friend and I went on an adventure that year. We worked together to make science magic and trips around the world. It was a wonderful year, and I continue to enjoy and share the joy of discovery with my students.

If the only people we allow into our sphere of influence are those who never challenge us, then we remain the same. We don't grow. We don't become the best we could be. The same is true when we surround ourselves with only negative naysayers.

A STORY FROM ALLISON KLINKE

First Grade Teacher

Some teachers know they want to move into leadership roles. I have never been that teacher, and never thought I would be. With each year of teaching, I've slowly gained confidence in my role as an educator and leader. This has led me to seek more opportunities and to have an impact larger than my classroom setting. What's helped the most is the support I have received from fellow teachers and administrators allowing me to grow and helping me realize the things I am truly capable of. It has also encouraged and pushed me to leave my comfort zone and step into roles that I never thought I would have been able to fulfill. This year has brought several new opportunities for me to have a leadership role with a greater impact on my campus.

Over the summer, we received the application to apply for a team leader position. I wasn't sure I wanted this role. I didn't quite know if I was ready to be leading a team. With the encouragement of my team members, I hesitantly submitted my application, thinking it unlikely I would be chosen. Then I received the email telling me I would be team leader this year! Instantly I was petrified, but at the same time excited, for this new role. I have definitely already enjoyed leading my team and being the liaison between our team and our administration. It's so funny now how I'm able to realize that I did have the ability to step into a leadership role, and I'm so grateful to those who recognized that potential in me.

Also, at the end of last year, I asked Nesloney about the possibility of starting student council on our campus. I thought it would be a great way to recognize student leaders and encourage others to follow their examples. When I approached him about this, I wanted to help and be involved with student council, but never thought I would start and lead it! Though I had no clue what I was doing, or getting myself into, I knew that starting student council would be beneficial to the kids we serve at Webb Elementary. Well, let me tell you, it has definitely been a challenge for me to step outside of my comfort zone and into this role, but I want our kids to know anything is possible when you're willing to take risks. Starting our first-ever student council has been a learning process for me and the students involved. We have had a few meetings, held elections for offices, and students were able to vote to decide who their leaders would be. While we are only in the beginning stages, I am already so proud and impressed by the students who showed initiative in applying for student council, including those who ran for an officer position. In watching the joy and excitement as the students gave their speeches then accepted their positions after voting, I realize that I'm excited to see where this road takes all of us.

Looking back, I never imagined myself being brave enough, or feeling worthy enough, to be a leader. But because I have those people in my life who are pushing me, and believing in me even when I don't, it has taught me so much about myself. We all need those people.

Find your people, those who will push you to be better than you dreamed. Find people who will help you remember who you are. They might be online, or they may be right down the hall. Wherever they are, take that first step and reach out. They're waiting.

THINGS TO CONSIDER

- Who are you helping to grow as an educator? How do you push them to be better?
- What does your support system look like? Is it an echo chamber? How do your people challenge you?

Tweet your answers and tell your story at #KidsDeserveIt

CHAPTER 27

LOOPING

I remember my second year of teaching very fondly. I was working at a school that served pre-kindergarten through fourth grade, and it felt like I was finally starting to get my feet on the ground. In January of that year, the district announced it was going to pull fifth grade down from the middle schools and move it back into the elementary schools.

A few months before school ended, I was asked if I would consider moving to fifth grade for the upcoming year. I would keep my same homeroom kids, a practice I later learned was called "looping."

I had never heard of looping but loved the idea of getting to know a group of kids and their parents even better.

A STORY FROM MARYLEE ARGUETA

Assistant Principal

Before becoming an assistant principal at Webb, I had been teaching for nine years in the classroom. During these nine years, I have had the opportunity to teach pre-kindergarten, kindergarten, first grade, and second grade, and, over the course of these years, I was able to get an understanding of what looping was all about with various students. When I first moved from pre-k to kinder with many of my students, I was nervous about a new curriculum. At the same time, I was excited for the new challenge, which was to create lifelong readers.

During teacher in-service for that school year, I will never forget that the other bilingual teacher and I received our rosters, and we each had thirty students. I began to panic and wonder how I was going to fit that many students in my classroom. Having some of my students the year before took away my fear of having to meet thirty new families. I wasn't sure what to expect in kinder, but I quickly learned it was night and day from pre-k. With thirty children for the first ten weeks of school and no naptime, there was never a dull moment.

Even though we were squished like a can of sardines, we created lifelong memories through singing, dancing, painting, creating, reading, jokes, funny voices, brain breaks, and playing during those ten weeks. I came every day with a smile on my face and ready for the adventure. We all know that each day has a hidden surprise in education— especially with the younger students. Needless to say, I was super sad when the principal announced a teacher had been hired, and I would lose ten kids. I didn't want them to leave. They were already part of my kindergarten classroom family! The part about this group of students that amazes me now is that they are going to be in sixth grade next year, and they still remember having me as their teacher. One of the students who had to move to the new class constantly tells me, "It's not fair that I had to get another teacher in kindergarten. I wanted to stay with you!" Another student I had my first year of teaching said, "My sister is lucky because she got to have you for pre-k and kindergarten." Those are the moments that make teaching worthwhile for me because I know in my heart I was able to connect with those students and create lasting memories.

My students, also known as "my kids," are my world, and I strived to be that teacher who made a lasting impact on their education. One way I left an imprint on my students was through reading. For me, reading is a passion, and I tried to instill that same joy with my students by using big books, puppets, role playing, different voices, and guest readers. One of the joys of looping with students is getting to see their personalities shine over the course of two years. I saw them shine not only in school but also outside of school. Parents were excited to invite me to soccer games, birthday parties, and older siblings' *quinceañeras*. The only hard part about looping is, at the end of the second year, the students and I were extra emotional. We cried like little babies on the last day of school. Over the years, I continued to stay in contact with students and parents due to teaching younger siblings of past students. Meet the Teacher night is always my favorite night because many of my past students come back and give me the biggest hugs and say, "Do you remember when I was in your class?"

Out of all the students from my first year of teaching kindergarten who come back to visit me, there is one student in particular who always melts my heart. His mother was battling cancer that year, and I became close to the family. I went to visit the mom in the hospital a couple of times during the end of her fight. I will never forget the private conversation we had during my last visit. She began to thank me for loving and caring for her son and said it meant the world to her. To this day, I clearly remember her telling me, "Please take care of him for me and give him the love of a mother because he doesn't ever stop talking about you and how much he loves you." This just broke my heart to pieces because I knew this sweet boy was about to lose his mother. After his mother had passed away, I remember him telling me on the last day of school, "You're never going to forget me, right?" I responded back to him, "No, *mijo* (son), you will always be in my heart!" His father and he always make it a point to stop by on Meet the Teacher night. The look on his face when he sees me is priceless! These are the moments that remind me why I chose this profession. Education is not solely about teaching students a curriculum. It goes hand in hand with building a bond with students and families that will follow them through their educational journey.

Positive Impacts of Looping

- Creates a strong bond between parents, teachers, and students
- Removes the anxiety and pressure over the first day of school for everyone
- Makes teachers familiar with the students' strengths and weaknesses
- Allows intervention to happen early with struggling students

- Makes parents familiar with the teacher's teaching style
- Encourages parent involvement because they have come to trust the teacher
- Allows students to know the teacher's rules and expectations from day one
- Gives students the sense of a family bond with classmates

I will never forget the class I looped with. My second year of teaching, I had a class full of wonderful, loving, active, funny, and caring students. We bonded deeply. I always pride myself in the relationships I try to build with my students. When I got to loop with this group, I was excited and terrified! I was excited because I'd get another year with these kiddos I had really grown attached to but terrified because a whole new curriculum was gonna be tough!

A STORY FROM ALEX COWDEN

Fourth Grade Teacher

This is my fourth year of teaching, but I have had the same group of kids three times. I taught them in first and second grade then let them have third grade without me (they needed to spread their wings); and now I am teaching them reading and social studies in fourth grade. I have a super strong connection with this group. I mean, of course, I have a strong connection with them. I've taught them for three years now, but what some people don't know is that the group I had my first year of teaching saved me.

My first year of teaching, I was a first grade teacher and thought I was exactly where I was meant to be. My mom had taught first grade for twenty years, and I was following in her footsteps. I had all of my mom's first grade things from her classroom, great ideas, and that new teacher spirit running through me. I was nervous, of course, but I was confident I had what it took to change the world—or at least that first grade classroom.

I worked hard during my student teaching experience, but I believe nothing truly prepares you for the realities of your own classroom and your first teaching job. However, things weren't just hard for me at school my first year. Things were hard at home, in my personal life. My grandmother, who was diagnosed with dementia that same year, went to the ER several times, and I would drive to Waco because I lived the closest. My Papaw, in Houston, was slowing becoming paralyzed and had to have surgery to remove a tumor. A relationship that I thought was headed to marriage (we have been married almost a year now) was going through a very rocky time. Typical life things, but they all slammed me at once. Hard. Somehow I kept those things completely separate. I don't know why or where I learned how to compartmentalize things that way, but that's what I did. At home I was hurting, but at school, I could shove all of that aside, teach, and be with my kids.

My partner teacher, my classroom, and my kids were my constant. They gave me life every single morning when I walked in. Yes, I was exhausted every day. There were struggles with each new day, but they gave me energy and life.

At the end of the year, I found out there was a second grade position open, and I went to my new principal, Todd Nesloney, and tried to tell him all of the reasons I should have that second grade position. He called me that afternoon and said yes! I was thrilled. I student taught in second grade, so I thought this was going to be my grade, and as an added bonus, I got my first group of kids back. No, I didn't do the traditional looping and have all of the same students in my room, but I did get hugs from them every day.

I did two years in second grade. I always thought that I was a younger grade teacher, and I loved this new group. Yes, every class is different, but I was getting to experience a new group, and every group of kids is so drastically different. I don't know how anyone can ever get bored with teaching because these kids keep you on your toes!

At the end of my third year of teaching and my second year in second grade, I was asked to go to fourth grade reading. My initial feeling was fear. I had never taught in a STAAR tested grade. All of these thoughts started whizzing around in my head. It's a whole different ball game. Will I be able to handle the older kids? But even with all of that going around in my head, I really wanted it. I really wanted to be in fourth grade reading. I went home and talked it over with my husband. He immediately said, "Yes, you should." He actually brought something to my attention that I hadn't even thought of . . . I'd already had that group. Twice. I had an upper hand on the relationships.

I have always worked really hard to build good, solid relationships with my students. If you have that relationship, those kids will move mountains. But when you work with a group multiple times, you have an even deeper connection. These students feel like they are my kids. I had relationships with their parents, know siblings, backgrounds, who they are related to, what they like or don't like, and their fears before they ever walked through my doors this year. As a teacher, building relationships with your students is in the job description and is honestly my favorite part! But knowing a student for four years, having them multiple times, and being able to watch them grow from first grade to fourth grade is truly amazing.

I already know that the end of this year is going to be hard. I have to send my babies to fifth grade, and I'm not going with them. It's time for them to fly without me and for me to fly without them. I have found my place, my grade, my niche. It might have taken me four years and three different grade levels to find it, but I wouldn't change those years for anything.

———

I can honestly say, though, that looping was one of the best things I've ever done. The only downside for me in looping with my students was how unbelievably hard it was to tell them goodbye the next year as they moved on to junior high.

I never like to say I had a "favorite" class because all of my classes have meant something special to me. But that group of students I got to loop with will forever hold a unique place in my heart—one that can never be forgotten. And watching many of them walk across the stage and graduate high school last year was another moment of pride I will not soon forget.

THINGS TO CONSIDER

- Is looping something you could consider doing? If you haven't yet considered it, what could be holding you back?

- How could looping with your students help you build stronger relationships with them and, in turn, also grow them more academically?

Tweet your answers and tell your story at #KidsDeserveIt

CHAPTER 28

CELEBRATING BECOMING

Who we are now is not who we were meant to be. The same could be said of who we were ten years ago or even ten weeks ago.

We are ever-changing, ever-growing, ever-learning people.

I have never been of the belief that people can't change. Maybe it's naive, but I choose to believe that people are capable of making enormous strides.

I often think about the teacher I imagined myself becoming, and then I compare that to the teacher I became in my first year. I look back on even last year—as a third-year administrator—and see all the ways I have grown, all of my failures and successes. Sometimes we make progress quickly, but often it takes time. When you're working with children, change can take a while, and the seed you plant now might not begin growing until many years later.

That's why it's so important for us to celebrate who we are becoming. It's important for us to realize our story is never finished and we get to write our own chapters. We don't have to let our circumstances take the pen from our hand and write our story for us. We get to write it.

And though we will all experience our own forms of despair, challenges, successes, celebrations, and more, each of those moments help shape us. They never define us. Who we become is completely up to us. And it's important that we teach that same lesson to our students—that we help them see they can be more than who they are in one of those moments.

A STORY FROM CAROLYN HAFLEY

Special Education Teacher

Helen stood in the doorway clutching her mother's hand. Her downcast, iridescent blue eyes did not meet the teacher's eyes as the mother explained that Helen exhibited selective mutism. She had the capacity to speak, but she only engaged in conversation occasionally. This beautiful auburn-haired girl was shy and reluctant to join the other students in any activity. The teacher worked incessantly to engage Helen in not only verbalization but also in play. As the year progressed, Helen was evolving or becoming. She would interact with the students by pointing and silently laughing. It was fun to observe her as she teased fellow students. She was so dramatic in her actions. It was wonderful to watch a devoted and optimistic teacher persevering in her endeavor to aid Helen's communication. As a teaching assistant that year, I observed the resoluteness and determination of the teacher as she tried many strategies and interventions. Each day before leaving, Helen had her one-on-one language time where she could share verbally. No verbalization occurred until the last day of school. As she scooted out the door, Helen spoke her name. What a beautiful voice!

This experience was instrumental in my "becoming" a teacher. As teachers, we are focused each day on helping students to reach their potential. The teacher and I had witnessed Helen's growth and her dramatic ability to communicate, but we also had developed as educators and individuals. Helen had contributed to our "becoming." Do we take the time to reflect on this process? As a young girl, I was constantly questioned about what I wanted to become when I was older. I thought it was a destination or a goal, but I discovered that becoming what you are meant to be is a process. It is a continuous course or journey with so many opportunities.

Two years ago, I joined the staff at John C. Webb. It was a new beginning for most of the staff. Mr. Nesloney had been appointed principal. The district had just redrawn attendance lines within the district. While most of the staff had never worked together, it was not long before new relationships were forged. This year one can perceive the importance and the significance of the "becoming" process. Forming relationships with staff members, students, and parents while learning and developing new techniques and surveying information from different sources has indeed contributed to that process. Mr. Nesloney communicated and conveyed a vision for the school that included an emphasis on developing relationships and communicating that each individual is important. The school motto is "You matter."

Each day at Webb Elementary, we are given an opportunity to make a difference in the lives of students. We get to celebrate their successes and support the students who face challenges. This year students had the opportunity to experience camaraderie by being a member of a house. Students from various grade levels were grouped together. They were able to develop new relationships by having opportunities to work together. The spirit of teamwork was celebrated and voiced while applauding and encouraging members of other houses. Students were able to interact and strengthen their interpersonal skills. It was indeed heartwarming to witness the scene of students encouraging one another regardless of their ages or abilities.

Why is there such an emphasis upon developing relationships at John C. Webb? The relationship that is formed is instrumental in that child's becoming. At the essence of the relationship is the human heart, which communicates love and acceptance. I am reminded often of Helen and how important the relationship is in the process of becoming. It was the beginning of a "beautiful voice." It is vital that a person take time to celebrate his or her successes and embrace the trials or challenges because you will be strengthened as you continue on your journey of becoming. I encourage you to reflect upon the people, events, and experiences that have helped you to become the wonderful person who will challenge and assist others in their journey of becoming.

Who are you becoming? Have you let the trials of this world control your actions and beliefs? Or have you made the decision to rise above, to be more, to be better? Every day it is a choice. It's not something completed in a day or single moment.

My hope is for you to unlock the chains that have held you to certain beliefs about yourself and see over the horizon to who you can truly become.

THINGS TO CONSIDER

- What limiting beliefs about yourself are holding you down?

- How are you celebrating the person you are now and not the person you once were?

Tweet your answers and tell your story at #KidsDeserveIt

CHAPTER 29

CLASSROOM TRANSFORMATIONS

In *Kids Deserve It!*, I wrote about my experience with classroom transformations. I talked about listening to the stories of Kim Bearden and then reading Dave Burgess' *Teach Like a Pirate*. I too wanted to transform my classroom. I built the Nez Hospital, and, to this day, students still message me about that one experience.

Adam and I also wrote about being careful that the lessons you design aren't all glitter but ones that have some meat to them. Far too often, teachers share these adorable activities and creations. They look incredible, but when you dive down into them, you realize they're all fluff. We have to remember that our job is to educate children—not help them create something cute.

How often do we get caught up in the excitement of designing a great activity or space but later learn it changed nothing about the way our students learn? It's important to be creative, but that creativity must also have substance. For that to happen, we must think and plan in new and different ways.

No longer do our students learn best from textbooks, art projects, desks in rows, or a lecture at the front of the room. They learn best by getting their hands dirty. They want the teacher there as part of the process, but they want to take charge too!

A STORY FROM ANDREA DAY
First Grade Teacher

When it comes to teaching, you have to think outside the box. You need to think of ways to make learning fun and engaging for the kids, to find a way to give them experiences that they wouldn't ordinarily have. A great way to do this is through a classroom transformation. The opportunities are endless! Some of the transformations I have done so far are Cloudy with a Chance of Meatballs, We are Pirates, Camping, and Winter Wonderland. With each one of these transformations, the kids were in awe. I had 100 percent engagement and almost no behavior issues.

When creating your transformation, you have to be creative. I would suggest enlisting the help of your fellow teachers, family, friends, and parents of students to get the supplies that you need. Transforming a classroom can be stressful, but it is all worth it in the end.

When I did the camping transformation, I paired up with another first grade teacher on my team. We decided that we wanted to go all out to give the kids a true camping experience. We contacted friends, family, and a few of our students' parents to collect everything we needed to turn the classroom into a true campground. We set up a large tent, put blue butcher paper down for a lake, had a real full-size kayak with paddles and life vests, had a picnic table, fake campfire, hammock, and more. The kids were in awe when they walked in the door. We spent the day at "Camp Day" and learned so much!

When planning a transformation, be sure to tie in what you are teaching. For example, when I did the camping transformation, I had the kids rotate through the different areas of the campsite. When they went to the lake, they would take turns fishing for sight words from inside the kayak and from the shore. Once they had caught three sight words, they wrote sentences using each word and then threw the fish back in. In the tent, I had sleeping bags, lanterns, lap desks, and pillows. The kids had books about camping, and they had to read the story and answer questions about what they read. They loved using the lanterns and head lamps for this task! Once they left the tent, they rotated to the campfire, where they roasted marshmallows to complete addition and subtraction problems. From there, they went to the hammock area where they used their binoculars, made from empty toilet paper rolls, to search for things around the campsite. Once they found an item, they marked it off their lists. At the picnic table, they looked at cards with different pictures and had to build what they saw using pretzel sticks and marshmallows.

There were times throughout the day when we all came together to read "scary" camp stories. I made sure to turn the lights out and have only the campfire and the lanterns going. We ended our day making one of my all-time favorite camping snacks—dirt in a cup. We had to read the recipe and follow the steps to make it. When I asked the kids to look back and reflect on their day, their faces were beaming. They were so excited and could not stop talking about their experiences. I still have kids pass me in the hall or see me out at duty and ask if I remember the day I took them camping. That right there tells me it was all worth it!

Perhaps a classroom transformation isn't your cup of tea, but you do want to step outside of your comfort zone and do it—because it's for the kids. If this is you, listen up. You do not have to do a huge, all-out transformation. You can keep it simple and get the same results and enthusiasm from your kids. For instance, my We Are Pirates transformation was not extravagant. I worked with a fellow teacher, and she and I dressed up like pirates and ordered hats and eye patches for the kids. Our activities were hands-on and tied in to what we were learning at the time. One activity that was a huge hit was a bin of sand that had "pirate booty" in it with math problems that the kids had to find and then solve. The biggest hit was giving the kids directions to create their own treasure map. They had to follow their map to find the treasure chest. This activity took us around the school and eventually landed us out on our playground where the treasure chest was waiting. Inside, we found more "pirate booty" and ten extra minutes of recess!

With classroom transformations, there is no right or wrong. Your only limits are the ones you put on yourself. If you aren't sure, start off small. For the more ambitious, go big. As teachers, we are known for borrowing ideas from each other and putting our own twist on them. You can find lots of fantastic educators on Twitter, Facebook, Instagram, and other social media platforms to follow and get ideas from. Reach out to these people and ask questions. Don't be shy to ask because our kids deserve it!

Now, don't get me wrong, classroom transformations are a lot of work. I love the advice that Kim Bearden and Hope King gave me, and that was, "Don't try to do too many!" The first time I did a classroom transformation, I did just one the entire year. And then the next year, I tried two.

Dollar stores are your best friend when designing transformations as well as asking friends and family like Andrea mentioned above. Another thing we've done as a campus is designated one empty classroom on campus as our "Transformation Room." So often when some of our teams of teachers wanted to do transformations, they worked together to transform all of their rooms. That was a ginormous undertaking. Now, when a team (or couple of teachers) want to work together on a transformation, they can use the transformation room and just transform one space. Then throughout the week they each take turns taking their class in there for a day of hands-on learning. It has really helped lighten the load!

We all know our kids learn best when they're actively engaged in the learning. We also know that memories stick with us when there's an emotional attachment to the memory. If we want to provide learning experiences for our students that will stick with them for more than just a few weeks, why not try out a classroom transformation that will leave them in awe. We owe it to our kiddos to go above and beyond for them.

THINGS TO CONSIDER

- In what new way can you transform your learning space?
- What is holding you back from taking a creative leap? How can you overcome that hesitation? Who can you bring along?

Tweet your answers and tell your story at #KidsDeserveIt

CHAPTER 30

SCARS

Sticks and stones may break my bones, but words will never hurt me. I've heard that old saying my entire life, but I've never understood its value. If there's one thing I'm sure of, it's that words do hurt.

Writing has always been a cathartic experience for me. It affords me the opportunity to communicate my thoughts much more clearly than if I were to express them verbally. It helps me to express what I know many will understand—that I am not perfect. I have never claimed to be someone who has it all together. Thanks to my personality type, I never feel as if I'm worthy of the recognition I've received for what I've accomplished.

Don't get me wrong—I'm not downplaying the good work that I have been a part of. I'm just saying I've never quite felt like I got it right. I'm also intensely reflective, always seeking feedback, wanting input, and identifying ways to improve.

Teachers are in a profession that allows for constant criticism. You all know what I'm talking about—that student who says you suck at life, the parent who says you don't know what you're doing, the colleague who complains about everything, and the administrator who makes you feel worthless.

But sometimes you get positive feedback. Maybe a caring co-worker shares ideas and resources to help you improve your lessons. Or maybe a parent takes you aside to thank you for doing a fantastic job. Those moments—those words—put gas in our tanks. They help us keep pushing along when the nights can feel so dark.

Then, thanks to bad timing, we are once again bombarded by the negative. I promise I'm going somewhere with this. I'm not just complaining. In *Kids Deserve It!*, I wrote about someone with whom I used to work, someone who left our team under very dark circumstances. After leaving, this person bombarded me constantly through social media, email, and texting about how I was a terrible person, how I clearly wasn't a Christian, how I do nothing right, and how I was only placed here to ruin lives.

It brought back memories of being in high school, being a student who never got in trouble, and one day being called to the office. I had run for student council representative my freshman and sophomore year and had been elected both years. So in my junior year, I decided to run for student council president. All three years running, I had used the exact same slogan, a slogan that my sarcastic, yet creative, mother came up with. What was that slogan? "Don't get your panties in a wad, vote for Todd."

Now I know what you might be thinking. Yes, it wasn't the most appropriate slogan, but my mom loved to push boundaries (I guess you can see where I get that from). Like I said, I had used that slogan my freshman year, sophomore year, and then my junior year. The day of the election, I remember (very vividly I might add) getting called down to the principal's office. The speeches and election were to take place in thirty minutes, so I wasn't sure why I was being called down.

I remember walking into the principal's office to see the principal seated at his desk and one of the assistant principals standing next to him. The moment I sat, their words washed over me like a tidal wave. "You, young man, must think you're pretty funny." I wasn't sure what they were talking about. So I sat there in shock, knowing I had never been in the principal's office for anything. Then he said, "We're here about your campaign slogan. You teenagers always think you are so hilarious, and you come up with these idiotic ideas. So tell us why did you come up with something as inappropriate as that?"

As I sat there, the only response I could think of was, "I didn't come up with it, my mom did." I then sat there as I was told, "You, son, are a loser, and this school doesn't want or need leaders like you. You will never be a leader in this school. Ever."

I couldn't believe what was happening. I couldn't believe the things they were saying to me. Up until this time, an adult had never spoken to me like that. Especially an adult who I viewed as someone I should respect.

I was then told that I was to go back to class. The speeches and voting would be delayed by one hour so they could mark my name off of every ballot. I would not be allowed to explain why it was happening, but I was to be present in the room when the voting and speeches commenced.

I stumbled back to my class, trying to comprehend what had happened. I remember sitting in the gymnasium an hour later. My friends were around me asking me what happened, and I couldn't even speak. After the voting took place, as students were finding their way back to class, I walked over to a school pay-phone, called my mom, and told her to pick me up. Immediately.

Though I knew the words they said weren't true, they have stuck with me to this day. Years down the road. And every time

I am feeling not so up-to-par, those words come sneaking back into my mind.

Then recently, I got to experience something like that again. Three anonymous sources shared some feedback with me. And it wasn't your typical feedback. It was extremely personal, deeply negative, and meant to cut to the bone. And it crushed me and brought back all of those memories from my junior year.

"When the principal sneezes, the whole school gets a cold." A phrase I often remember, I always take it to mean that, as the principal, I help set the tone for the school. My demeanor and attitude can leave ripples felt all day long.

So when I received the crushing feedback (right after spending four hours in a dunking booth), I closed my door and cried. I let it out. Then I sat there and remembered that my only option was to take what I could from their remarks, learn from them, and put them on the back burner for now while I go out there and be there for the kids.

So I left my office and went out into the school with a smile, with jokes, with hugs, and no one was any the wiser.

And what did I do later that afternoon and evening? I reached out to my support system, to people who would help me digest the information and not take it so deeply personal. And it wasn't easy. At first, I didn't want to tell anyone what was said about me. I was embarrassed. And on a crazy level, it brought up those memories from the past, and I sat there and thought, *Maybe all this venom is true.*

Then a week passed. And every word that was written was still fresh in my mind. It still hit me throughout the day and told me, "You're a loser," "No one likes you," "You do a terrible job," "You're a terrible person." And I know these things aren't true. I know it. But they're there.

And the funny thing? No one in my day-to-day work life (except my assistant principal Aaron) knew what I had read about myself. But the week was capped off with little reminders here and there from staff, from students, from parents, and from my own family who helped remind me of the worth I bring— who helped me refocus myself.

I share all of this for several reasons. Primarily, I want to offer some hope to those who are going through something similar. You are not alone. I also share my story to remind you to lean on others in times of despair. We can't do this alone. Without the support of my friends, I wouldn't have made it through.

Finally, I share this story to remind us all that words matter. Wounds inflicted by hateful speech aren't wounds that heal easily, and they often leave permanent scars. Feedback is important, criticism is important, and reflection is important, but there is a way to do that so we all grow better together.

We all have wounds. We all have scars. But we can let those scars be reminders that we were strong enough to survive. I have been guilty of saying or doing things I know have wounded someone else, and I have tried to make amends for those moments after I was made aware of them.

My encouragement and reminder to us all is to think through what we say and do before it's something we can't take back. If it's too late, if it's already out there, take the time to find that person and apologize. And mean it.

Scars don't ever disappear, but we can learn from the wounds and become better. So today, I choose to be better.

THINGS TO CONSIDER

- What scars are you still reflecting on that you need to move forward from?

- Think about your work relationships. Is there someone you need to talk to about wounds you might have inflicted?

Tweet your answers and tell your story at #KidsDeserveIt

CHAPTER 31

WEBB HOUSE SYSTEMS

If you've read *Kids Deserve It!* or follow any of my musings on social media, you know how big a fan I am of the Ron Clark Academy (RCA). I was able to visit there as a teacher many years ago and then recently as an administrator. For me, visiting the academy is like visiting Disney World. I just can't gush enough.

One thing RCA does that blows me away is its house system, which is loosely based after the houses in the Harry Potter novels. At RCA, every child and teacher is sorted into a house. They remain in that house during their years at RCA, and everything they do revolves around the house they're in. It's a fantastic system that really builds camaraderie, excitement, and energy in the students and staff alike.

When visiting RCA as an administrator, I knew the house system was one of the most important ideas to take back to my campus. After visiting the academy, I gathered my seven teachers and assistant principal, who had accompanied me on the visit, and the planning began!

One thing I love about social media and RCA is how many walls are torn down, thanks to the invention of platforms such as Twitter and Instagram. Before returning to RCA as an administrator, I had formed great relationships with several current and former RCA staff members, including Kim Bearden, Hope King, Adam Dovico, and Wade King. When we decided we wanted to take the leap into the house system, I reached out to Wade. He was such a great support with a wealth of ideas that really helped our school take this idea and run with it. The Ron Clark Academy app, as well as my buddy Chris Pombonyo, was also an incredible resource full of ideas that guided our decisions.

The first step we took was deciding on how many houses to have. RCA had only four houses, but they have far fewer students than we do. So at 750 or so kiddos, we decided on five houses. We didn't want to have so many houses that it might lose its flavor.

The next step was choosing colors for each house, a task that proved to be more difficult than you might think. We didn't want to choose any colors that were associated with our district colors. We wanted this to be totally unique and also didn't want to give any house an advantage by having a large chunk of their students with shirts of a certain color. Ultimately, we went with red, orange, yellow, green, and purple houses. We didn't name the houses because we wanted the full team at Webb to take part in that process. We did decide on the cultural or geographical region that each house would represent to help facilitate the naming process, but I'll shed more light on that in a bit. We also decided each house would have a house leader. During our first year, the house leaders were people who had been to RCA and could help guide the rest of their houses.

Our next hurdle was figuring out how to bring this to our school team so they wouldn't feel like it was one more thing on their plates. The other staff members hadn't been to RCA. They hadn't seen the magic in action. So we knew we had to share this new idea in a way that would eliminate barriers and bring the energy and fun from the first moment.

We headed to a local dollar store and party store to buy supplies, returning with tons of decorations in our five house colors. We dressed in wild outfits—I love my neon orange suit—that were also matched to our house colors. We turned on some party music, blew up a ton of balloons, rolled out the red carpet, and commenced to have fun. It was the first day we were all back together in August, and it was planned as a surprise celebration.

As staff entered the gym that day, they were greeted with a party unlike any we had thrown before. We had large buckets full of strips of paper with house colors written on them, and staff members had to reach in and draw to find their house. Then they went to that house's table, put on some face paint, and waited for everyone else to draw their house colors out of the buckets.

After getting everyone seated, I welcomed them and briefly explained our new house system. Right away, we noticed a mistake we had made. I really wanted to have an equal representation of every house in every grade level. By letting teachers just draw a house color out of a bucket, some grade level teams ended up with most of their people in the yellow house or purple house. So right away, we had to switch a couple of teachers to make sure every house had equal grade level representation. Then, we began again!

We started out talking about our goals for the houses and building a campus-wide team atmosphere—one not separated by grade level or classes. The idea was to create teams where kindergarten students worked alongside fifth graders. We had been using a CHAMPS system for behavior expectations but wanted something to add to it that had the kids feeling like they were part of something bigger than themselves.

The first thing we did was come up with house names. House leaders explained to their teams what geographical region or culture they represented, and then everyone worked together to name their houses. The red house, representing Asia, became Ganbaru, which means "tenacity." The yellow house, representing Native Americans, became Ohitika, which means "bravery." The orange house, representing Europe, became Enas, which means "we are one." The purple house, representing Africa, became Pendana, which means "house of love." And the green house, representing South America, became Bem-Vindos, which means "house of welcoming."

After the naming, we played three different "Minute to Win It" type games. They were light-hearted but provided quite a few laughs. We wanted to show the staff how fun this could be and how we were the gatekeepers inviting our students to have fun alongside us.

We explained to the staff that everything we were going to do this year would revolve around houses. No longer would we have fundraiser goals set by class or box top collections by grade level. Everything would be by houses. I hired a graphic designer from the website Fiverr who designed five separate House Crests. We put those crests on giant banners at the front of the school and even hired a local painter to paint the crests on the wall outside our cafeteria. Each house had t-shirts made with their crest and house name that students could buy and that we gave to every staff member.

All the students this first year were placed into the house that their homeroom teacher had been placed into. We did that to make things a little easier to understand and explain our first year taking this on. For all the years that follow, those kids and staff members will never switch house colors. The house they were first placed into is the house they'll always be in. Meaning that every year, as our kids move on and are mixed up more and more, the classrooms will have more and more houses mixed into them.

We were also going to be giving points to houses throughout the year. Our first year doing this, only administrators, camp (specials) teachers, custodians, and cafeteria workers were going to be giving out points. We used an app called Class Dojo that many teachers were already familiar with. Instead of creating a class of kids in Class Dojo, we created our five houses and shared the classes with all who were awarding points. We would give points for different character traits that we saw being exhibited by students or for a variety of other reasons—collecting box tops, fundraisers, attending after school events. Every Friday during the announcements, we would reveal which house was in the lead.

We also planned House Games the final Friday of every month. During each grade level's specials time, the PE teacher, Joni Leonard, would plan fun games that each grade level competed in as they came to her class. Every child was allowed to participate, and at the end of the day we brought the entire school together. At those house games, each house shared their specialized cheer or chant with the rest of the school, we played some kind of crazy game and always had lots of music and often a dance party! These house games lasted about thirty to forty-five minutes and were the highlight of each month.

Near the end of the year, we started giving our house games a theme. Our April game was a glow-in-the-dark and black-light party where we bought glow necklaces for everyone, blacked out all our windows, and put black lights all over the gym. In May we played a water game outside where everything had a beach feel.

At each house games, we would also announce which house won for that month. The kids were very interested in this part because they knew at the end of the first semester, the house with the most points would get a special field trip. And at the end of the school year, the house with the most points for the entire year also won a special field trip. So, essentially, the same house could go on a special field trip twice in one year. But if they won the points, they deserved it!

Our parent-teacher organization helped pay for our January field trip, while the school covered the May field trip. When choosing a trip, we wanted a place that would require the students to interact and work together. There was a local place, in a nearby city, called Horseshoe Junction. It was one of those places we could rent just for our students and had go-karts, miniature golf, indoor rock climbing, laser tag, bumper boats, and much more to keep them busy. When Pendana won for the first semester, every staff member came back from that field trip raving about how great it was. They said it was especially powerful to watch our fifth graders step up and take the kindergartners on a go-kart when the kinder kiddo was too short to reach the pedals or watch the third graders help the first graders with their mini-golf skills. It was a bonding experience that also proved to be a great deal of fun for the kids. When Bem-Vindos won for the year, they took the same trip and had the same reaction.

A STORY FROM JONI LEONARD

Physical Education Teacher

When I first heard of the new house games, I had a lot of emotions all at the same time. I was excited about how our students would earn points. I thought the idea of the kids seeing teachers could help earn points for their house was amazing, and our students would see that we were all working toward a common goal and having fun at the same time. My major concern was how our students would handle it if their house didn't win. I know competition is a part of the real world, and we talk about that with our students and teach them to have good sportsmanship, but, honestly, it is very hard sometimes.

Once we had talked with our students about the house games, it was time for all the teachers to get them pumped up and ready for the first-ever house games. The last Friday in the month was approaching fast, and the kids were asking what game they were going to play. We told them they would have to show up on Friday and find out. In a way, if felt like our students were counting down the days until we were going on vacation, but they actually were waiting to see what we had in store for them in the house games.

On the day of our first house games, I was excited to see our kids so pumped. We had students and teachers dressed from head to toe in house colors. We even had some that included the other house colors in their attire because we are all family. When I noticed that, I knew we had embarked on something very special.

The game field was set, and each house had their own place in the gym. When you walked into the gym on the last Friday in September, you could feel the exhilaration in the air. Our game for the day was a life-sized version of Hungry Hungry Hippos! If you walked past the gym, you would have thought all the students and teachers had jumped off the edge and gone crazy.

The gym looked very chaotic with students lying on their stomachs on top of a scooter and two other students holding onto the students' legs on the scooter. They were thinking outside the box on how they could get their teammate to the middle of the gym and back as fast as possible. We had teams put the smallest person on the scooter and some put the largest person, some were trying to push or pull the students while some were trying to swing them to the middle of the gym. We had people everywhere, and the laughter could be heard over the music. Students were cheering, chanting, and dancing their team on, and when the time was up, they all took part in helping count how many items the team had gathered. Each team cheered for the other color house as they announced how many pieces they gathered.

Soon it neared the part of the game I had been worried about. Each team could earn some points for their house, but we would only have one winner per grade level. I had already started to think out what I was going to say if we had anyone who was not being a very good sport toward the winners. I started announcing how many points each house earned, starting with the least amount and working my way up. When I announced the winning house, the house that won was cheering, and when they stopped I was waiting for the negativity to begin, but what I was not expecting is what happened next. One student got up and went over and started giving the others a high five for winning and within a few seconds we had the entire class helping the winning house celebrate. When they left the gym that day, they were just as excited as they were when they came in and were already asking what we'd do for the next game.

At the end of the day, when I finally had a chance to reflect on everything, I realized we'd had an amazing day, but we'd also taught our kids that it's okay to celebrate other people's victories instead of being resentful or trying to tear them down.

As with any new initiative, did it go perfectly? Heck, no! We learned more and more as we went along. We learned we had to set clear expectations for staff members of what their roles were during house games. We learned themed house games were way more fun but also required quite a bit more work and planning.

And the biggest question that might be looming in your mind—was there any pushback or did everyone buy in? The easiest way I can answer that is by sharing that it was really hard to not be a part of the house system or house games when you saw how truly transformative and fun it was for the kids. As at any school, there are some staff members who get into it far more than others. But during our end-of-year-surveys, when students shared that house games were their favorite part of the year, we knew we were onto something.

So if the house system is something that sounds interesting to you, my biggest advice is to visit the Ron Clark Academy. And if you can't, start by downloading the RCA app. It is full of amazing resources and tools that will help you on your way. I promise, if you jump full force into this, you won't regret it for a second. But you've got to be all in!

THINGS TO CONSIDER

- How can you create more of a collaborative and family environment at your school?
- How are you building up character traits in your students?

Tweet your answers and tell your story at #KidsDeserveIt

CHAPTER 32

WHEN YOU MARRY INTO EDUCATION

Spouses and family members are often the unspoken heroes in educators' lives.

They know what we go through every day. They know the sleepless nights and the hours spent in the classroom long after the children have left for the day. Spouses and family members live with us through the stress of evaluations, state testing, district mandates, difficult team members, and so much more.

The people who take care of us when we get home each day play a monumental role in our careers. They listen to our struggles, they give us a shoulder to cry on, and they love us in spite of ourselves.

It's not easy to be an educator's spouse. It's hard for them to watch the many hours we spend away from home taking care of someone else's children. If we're lucky, they understand that it's our calling, that we were meant for this.

When I thought about writing this book, I knew it had to include a story from my wife, Liz. She's not a staff member at Webb, but like so many spouses of teachers and administrators, she does more than her fair share of work at our school, attending events, setting up for events, and just keeping us company on a late night.

A STORY FROM LISSETTE NESLONEY
Principal's Wife

When you're married to an educator, I think you see things differently from those who aren't. I'm a wife of a teacher turned principal. When I met Todd, he was a fifth grade math teacher. I always loved stopping by his classroom any chance I got and watching the wonderful connection he had with his students and the awesome things they were doing. We'd go to baseball games on date nights to cheer on his students and also attend other extracurricular activities.

One of the reasons I fell in love with him was the passion he had for education and changing kids' lives. To this day, there are some students he keeps in contact with.

I still remember the day he told me about the offer he had received to be a principal and the district it came from. My anxiety immediately began to brew just thinking about the decision we would soon have to make and the changes it would bring. Things were great, I thought. There was no need to change things up, and the things Todd was currently doing in his classroom—Classroom Champions and many others— were amazing.

We talked about it at length, and we knew it would be a huge change to take on, but after much prayer, Todd knew this was what he was meant to do. I lost count of how many times

I asked him, even after he accepted the position, "Are you sure this is what you want to do?" I was afraid he would lose and miss that special connection he was so good at making with his students. Little did I know, or was ready for, the connections he would make on a much larger scale and the heartache that could also bring.

Teachers carry the weight of their students. Principals carry the weight of their teachers, students, and all of their staff. There are nights when Todd comes home after a long day, and I can see the worry on his face. I can sense the stress and defeat he feels when he is unable to help a student. I see the frustration he feels when people don't understand the behind-the-scenes battles he fights for his staff. Sometimes it's the feeling of defeat that comes from state testing scores that, no matter the positive things and the change a school is doing, always seem to define him and give him those negative feelings.

I've watched firsthand the stresses that education puts on a person. The hours outside of school spent grading, writing lesson plans, making parent phone calls, and more. Many people think teachers just show up, hang out with kids, and leave. If you're married to an educator, you know it's so much more. You also know the amount of emotional stress they take on and that many of them have a hard time talking about.

Even with all those challenges, four years later, I think Todd and I would agree that God knew what he was doing all along—of course! I've loved seeing the wonderful family Webb Elementary has become and the amazing things they are doing to make a difference in kids' lives.

But I will surely never forget the first year and some of the amazing teachers on that team—oh, and the bunny—who to this day still have a special place in my heart for sticking with Todd through the learning phase.

It wasn't an easy year. It was filled with tears, challenges, heartache, and so much more. But I think most would agree that it was all worth it. I don't get to stop in as much as I'd like anymore, as our lives have become incredibly busy, but you can bet you'll see me hanging out and seeing the awesome team at Webb Elementary any chance I get!

Being the spouse of an educator isn't easy. And there are other careers out there too that are just as difficult, if not more so. But I like to believe that our spouses are our unsung heroes for putting up with this crazy passion of ours for what others call a job.

And for those of you out there who don't have a spouse you go home to, you know that your friends, family, and personal learning network (PLN) play a huge role in keeping you sane. If you don't have someone, reach out online. None of us were meant to walk this road alone. We all need to find our people.

THINGS TO CONSIDER

- How has your spouse, a family member, or close friend supported you?
- How can you celebrate and thank them today for being your rock?

Tweet your answers and tell your story at #KidsDeserveIt

CHAPTER 33

FAITH

When I decided to write something after finishing *Kids Deserve It!*, I wanted to include a chapter that explored the idea of faith and the role it plays in my life and the lives of other educators.

A STORY FROM KEVIN HALIBURTON

Music Teacher

It was the summer of 2015, and I was diagnosed with low oxygen levels. I was told to go on disability and given an oxygen machine for the house and a portable one for travel. The last thing I wanted was for my principal to see me. To top it off, my wife and I lost our second child to our second miscarriage. I remember wondering how I was going to hide this oxygen machine from my boss. Through prayer, I removed the oxygen machine without the doctor's consent. My wife called everyone to talk me out of it. I knew if I had the faith the size of a mustard seed, God would get me through this. I visited my doctor before school began, and to everyone's amazement, the doctor laughed and told me I no longer needed the oxygen machine. I was free of that dilemma.

It was time to start my first year as the music teacher at Webb! But please keep in mind I had never taught elementary school. I was terrified because after teaching junior high for fourteen years and high school for six years, this was a new experience. I could not figure out why God assigned me to this school of tiny people. I remember during our open house many of the teachers, who had taught there for years, warned me about the behavior of the students.

God gave me a totally different vision. He showed me their futures. He showed me doctors, lawyers, athletes, and superstars. I saw children who needed love and guidance, diamonds that needed shining. I soon forgot about my situation, forgot about losing two children, and forgot about my health. A smile immediately formed as I met the students and their parents.

My smile quickly changed after my first week with . . . the kindergartners! The smile transferred to my wife who laughed daily. It was so bad the school custodian checked on me. It was as if the kindergartners knew beforehand I had never taught their grade level. But praise God for stickers! Match, set, point, I knew I had figured it out. I started to believe I could do it.

A few weeks later, I was introduced to a student who decided to transfer back during the middle of the school year. I could see the look of terror in teachers' eyes when he walked by. And when he walked down the school hall, it was like the parting of the Red Sea. Most people saw a troubled kid, but God showed me something different.

I am an ordained reverend. Many of my coworkers are not aware because I do my best to let my actions show my love for God. He has gifted me with the ability to work with children and tell if they can sing. I never heard this student sing, but I knew what he could do. That soon changed after my first class with him. My co-worker laughed at me when I told her my vision. I will admit, even I questioned God. This young man was in trouble constantly—in the principal's office and lunch detention on a daily basis.

One day I challenged him and shared with him my vision. He laughed and said, "Man, I can't sing!" I told him if I could teach him how to sing in fifteen minutes, he had to change his ways. He agreed to the challenge. I could see the class looking at me as if I had lost my mind. Within five minutes, the kid was singing. I told him if he followed me, his life would change. I asked him if he wanted to change. He looked at me and said, "Thank you for embarrassing me and picking on me."

I cried after his class left because I was beginning to see my purpose. The next day, that student walked up to me and apologized, telling me he wanted to learn. I shook his hand, told him I loved him, and could see the pain in his eyes. We rehearsed after school for a month. The teachers saw a quick change in his behavior. He began to encourage other students. The teachers were so proud of him. He shared many private stories about his family situation. You could see a different person emerging.

He sang at our black history program and received a standing ovation. His mother stood up with her mouth opened and cried. She was so proud of him. My wife called him her son. The next year, he moved in with his father and transferred to a different school. He returned toward the end of the fall, out of control. He asked me if he could sing in our choir, but I reminded him of our deal. He told me it was going to be hard. It hurt me seeing his old behaviors. I could see the pain in his eyes.

During the final week of school, he walked up to me, told

me that I was the closest thing he had to a real father and that he loved me. I thought about the time my health was bad and about losing two babies. I thought about my fears. I thank God for John C. Webb Elementary. I thank God for removing the oxygen tank and for the baby that my wife and I were able to welcome into this world in September. The same God in the valley is the same God on the mountain.

I remember reading Kim Bearden's book, *Crash Course*, and there being a chapter about how her faith has shaped her and who she is. Then I attended a conference where my good friend Wade King was speaking, and at one point, he shared a similar story. I wanted to share my own faith story in my first solo book.

Faith has been a big part of my life for as long as I can remember. After my parents divorced when I was going into junior high school, my mom had us in church all the time—from Sunday morning service to Wednesday night youth group to all sorts of activities in between. My youth, and who I am today, was shaped by the relationships built during that time of my life. The two youth ministers I had, Nick Shock and Troy Sikes, are two men I give full credit to for helping me walk through those formative years and always setting a great example of what a man looked like.

I don't know that I would be where I am today without faith, that belief in something greater than myself. For me, it's the belief that someone would create me, send his son to die for me, and forgive all the sins I commit on a daily basis. Prayer is also a large part of my life. Taking time to pray about every decision and really seek God's will is something that plays into everything I do. I've seen firsthand the power of prayer. I've watched my own life be transformed through prayer, and those moments when someone will say a prayer over you are indescribable.

A STORY FROM SHERRI DESERN
Pre-Kindergarten Teacher

It's hard sometimes to keep the faith, have hope, and leave life's troubles in the car, but I do my best every day. The kids I teach have so many troubles in their own lives; they surely don't need mine too!

I always remember that we were each created in God's image. I once read an article that talked about what would happen if we kept that thought at the forefront of our minds, of being created in God's image, when working with children. Each child is created in God's image. Yes! Even that one who drives you up the wall. He or she is still created in the image of God. That means they are special. That means you are special. We are all special, and we all deserve to be here, so why not make life worth living?

Let's enjoy our time together. Yes, we all have ups and downs, but I believe that God has brought us together with the kids we teach on purpose. There is a reason we are their teacher. Now, make the best of it. Pray about it and do your part to make that student, every student, feel special and loved. Even on the days that you don't think they deserve it, they really do!

I teach pre-K, so sometimes I wonder if the students will remember me when they get older. I never forget my purpose with them, though. Even if they don't remember me, I can always make sure that they remember my example. I do my best to model each day how to be polite and use manners. I use kind words. I show how to care for others. I show how to practice consideration for others.

And even though my students might not remember my face or my name when they grow up, I sure hope they remember my example—knowing that happiness can come from when we serve others and give of ourselves to a higher calling.

I went back and forth over whether or not to include this chapter in the book. Why? Because I view myself as someone who is welcoming to people from all walks of life. I've always prided myself on not being judgmental and truly being able to see someone and respect someone for who they are. I didn't want this chapter to give anyone the wrong idea. I didn't want them to think, "Oh, look at him. He thinks his faith is better than what I choose to believe or not believe in!" or "I guess if we don't have faith in something, we can't be a good educator." That's not it at all! I'm sharing this side of myself because I believe in sharing all of my story.

As an educator, our jobs are so very hard. There are so many days filled with doubt, overwhelming thoughts, heartbreak, and workloads that seem to want to break our backs. That is where my faith has come into play. I believe God has everything planned perfectly for me. But that doesn't mean I get an easy road, and it doesn't mean I will always understand what is happening. What it does mean is that I have a heavenly Father who is helping guide my steps and is always looking out for me.

My faith is who I am. It's a part of me, and it's a part of me I wanted to share with you.

A STORY FROM GERALDINE WILLIAMS
Third Grade Teacher

"Lord, what are you saying now? I trust you, and I want to fulfill your will and purpose for my life." My faith and trust in God is everything to me! It is how I survive my day-to-day life. Truthfully, there are some days when I feel like my back is against the wall and there is no way out. I have surrounded myself with frogs in my classroom to remind me to Fully Rely On God. There is absolutely no way I would be sane if I didn't trust and rely on God in everything I do.

Three years ago, I was basically without a job due to our school district making some changes. I didn't know what God was saying to me because I knew that he had placed me here in Navasota. I knew I was supposed to work with and help the children of this community, but I was now facing this situation. Confused and weary, I cried out to Him, "Lord, I want to be where you want me to be and do what you want me to do. I won't move or make a decision without hearing from you! I'd rather be slow to move than to move and be outside of your will." In order to do that, you have to have a relationship with God and faith that he will come through for you. God answered and placed me at John C. Webb Elementary School. I have to admit, I was a little worried because I would now be working with the little babies, but I never doubted it was where I was supposed to be.

Being where God wants you does not mean you stop using your faith because you are where you are supposed to be. You have to constantly rely on his guidance to direct your walk and talk every day.

As much as you love and trust God, working in the school system will certainly test that faith. Stress on teachers and administrators to meet state requirements is at the top of the list. The lack of support and drive from parents to make the best decisions to help their children be successful in school is next on the list. If you're not careful and you don't pray about what you say and do, you will make serious mistakes and hurt the very ones who need you the most.

I believe the most difficult or challenging children need more love and understanding than the average kid. We have so many babies who fit into this category. They are hurting and don't have anyone to believe in them. Because they are this way, they come to us acting out in many different ways. In order for us to give them the love and attention they need, we have to look past what is on the surface and push beyond what we can see to help them. You can only do that with the help of God and your faith in Him to give you that extra strength, love, and guidance for each individual who needs it.

My take on faith is the belief that something will be done or happen, even though you can't see it happening. You see I believe that I will help every child that comes in contact with me in one way or another. I not only teach school lessons; I teach life lessons. Being a teacher is not an eight-to-five job. You're in it to make a difference in the lives of children year after year. When you are affecting the lives of others, you want to make sure you do it right, with love and care. You have to have faith that you can make a difference, even if it does not seem like you can. You may not see the results of all that you put in, the child may not show their gratitude, and neither might seem worth it. Your faith will let you know that you are fulfilling the purpose for your life and the lives that are meant to cross your path.

I have faced many struggles in my personal life and at school that have caused me to stand on my faith. I've had multiple family members who were very ill, which required me missing multiple days from work. It was very difficult to fulfill my obligations at work, as well as my personal responsibilities to my family at home. Some days I would come in tired, frustrated, and overwhelmed. Financially, I didn't know if I would make it. All I had to hold on to were my purpose and my faith that God would see my family and me through it all.

This year was really rough for many of our staff members. As I stated above, there were staff members who had hard times, sickness, and even the deaths of loved ones. Though there were individuals who would often pray for one another, we didn't come together as a collective group to do so. There was a Bible study created that allowed those of us who wanted to come together to learn of God and his way of approaching the different trials that would come our way. This was such a blessing. We were able to share in the hurts and struggles of our co-workers and support them through prayer. We were able to stand in the gap and believe in their situation being worked out. It was a great feeling to know you had an administration, as well as a faculty and staff, who were believers and wanted to walk in the will of God.

Faith is so very personal to each and every individual. What I've learned is that my faith plays a huge part in the man I am today. It guides my decisions, provides me with hope, and helps me conquer those dark nights.

THINGS TO CONSIDER

- What role does faith play in your life and day-to-day job as an educator?
- How can we take the time to educate ourselves on the faith of others and respect their beliefs as well?

Tweet your answers and tell your story at #KidsDeserveIt

CHAPTER 34

MEANT TO BE

There are so many times in our lives when we're faced with a difficult decision. Do we take that promotion? Do we look at purchasing a new home? Can we afford a new car? Are we ready to have children? Man, being an adult is tough! But what I love most is this: Even when you're in the midst of making a decision, even when you're not quite sure of what you're supposed to do, the pieces still fall right into place.

A STORY FROM JENNIFER SHORT
Assistant Principal

Just one year prior to coming to Webb, I began working on an administration certification that, little did I know, would change my families' lives forever. My certification program required me to spend several days shadowing a principal in order to get the sense of what "a day in the life of an administrator" would be like. This opportunity was not granted to me on

277

my home campus, for reasons I do respect. This gave me the opportunity to design my own observation experiences. Not knowing what my future in administration held for me, I began shadowing principals of multiple levels and in different areas. For example, this ten year kindergarten through second grade teacher spent a day experiencing the vandalizing, adult-wan-na-be, attitudinal, and dress-code-violating school day that is junior high school. After broadening my understanding of "True Life: I'm a Public School Administrator," I wanted to seek experience in a district outside of my own.

After reading the book *Kids Deserve It!* and having followed and been inspired for years by Todd Nesloney's passion for bettering kids' lives and the roles teachers play in them, I knew visiting his school was a bucket list must. I felt blessed to have been given the opportunity to shadow him for a day and just witness the impact he and his staff have on their students.

This dizzying, yet self-affirming day is still a blur to me, but I will do my best to hit the highest of the highlights. I spent the morning getting the greatest calf burning workout known to man by being a part of the entire campus' goings-on. Seriously, I had to have hit at least 10,000 steps within the first hour and a half as I followed Mr. Nesloney all over the campus! I saw so many great things happening and tried to participate in as much as I could. The teachers, staff, and students were so welcoming and were very comfortable with my questions and participation.

Midway through the day, my questions to Todd and our subsequent discussions led to him mentioning that he was hiring a new assistant principal. While I was aware of this and did fill out an online application, I had only brought a copy of my resume for him to look over and critique. He then nonchalantly stated,

"Maybe we could have an interview today." Now, wanting to come across as confident, I simply replied, "Sure!" trying to keep my cool. He then sent me out to visit classrooms on my own and take notes on anything I saw. As I traveled around to several classrooms, I honestly wasn't thinking that this impromptu interview was actually a possibility. When I returned, I walked into a conference room where Todd and his then assistant principal, Aaron Marvel, were sitting with copies of my resume and open laptops, which I could only assume were to be used to play a note-taking game of "Jennifer's Career Hangman."

I honestly have no recollection of this blurred portion of the day, but it must have gone well because I was then asked to stay after school to sit in front of a panel of teachers. The panel portion of my interview was something I thoroughly enjoyed. After an hour of real conversation with these teachers, I felt connected to their passion and drive to better the campus culture and climate there at Webb Elementary. Oh, and by the way, the teachers and I talked so long that Todd ditched me to attend another engagement. After saying our goodbyes and thanking them for their time, I exited the room and, as the door slowly closed behind me, I heard voices saying, "Wow," and "That is not what I had expected"—leaving me with both a sense of hope and a nail-biting, every-word-analyzing sense of angst.

Shortly thereafter, I received a phone call from Todd and was asked to join this awesome team as Webb Elementary's newest assistant principal!

Prior to this change, I had spent my entire ten-year teaching career in the same school district; I even completed my student teaching hours within this same district. My children attended this school with me, knowing my family of colleagues, and had only been accustomed to life with a teacher-mom. So the next step was to introduce this plan of change to my boys. Two out of the three boys were not fazed, while one spent the entire summer before our school move showing signs of hesitation. New school, new town, new grade, and mom in a new role. With all this to take in, I expected some reservations from the boys.

Once school had begun, our little family of four was met with a very different school culture than we had grown accustomed to. Where we came from, our one-income family was most definitely not among the wealthiest of families but was among the majority race population. Here at Webb, my boys were in the minority as white Caucasian students. Because of the population that Webb Elementary served, now my boys' financial opportunities matched that of several of their peers. I began closely watching and listening to my children from day one. I wanted to be ready to answer any questions and help them feel at ease with the different look of this school's population. With the twins being first graders and the youngest being in kindergarten, I was anticipating lots of discussions about how different people can look and how that doesn't affect who they are. Previously, these boys had only been in classes with other Caucasian children and a couple of students who were of mixed race, due to the populations that our previous school served.

After several weeks of closely monitoring my boys' reactions, I began to feel ashamed of myself. As I listened to my boys come home with silly, enjoyable stories about all of their classmates, I was disappointed in the fact that I doubted my parenting and thought that my boys would see skin color before someone's personality or character. As a former ESL and dual language teacher who worked hard to help provide my Hispanic students the best education I could give them, I was upset with the fact that I didn't trust in the innocent and kind hearts of my three young boys. I then began to see that this school was providing better, more well-rounded social opportunities than they had ever had in their young lives.

While my mind was so closely focused on one unnecessary worry, I was failing to see some personal issues my one hesitant son was having. Coming from a divorce situation and being so young, one of the twins was not having the easiest time adjusting to all of these changes. Fortunately, his teacher and I caught onto his struggle and together we were working to support him in any way possible. Even after having to make some difficult adjustments that would help with his ability to cope with all the change, this talented and passionate teacher continued to provide my son with the best educational experience she could. It was easy to see that, after sharing our story with their teachers, the boys were wrapped in love and any concern I may have had was washed away.

I too have felt the undeniable feeling that Webb is where we are meant to be. Very rapidly I felt a strong connection to the teachers and staff. I joined the Webb team at the tail end of a very lengthy divorce process. At times, my personal life had gotten difficult and stressful. While all this was going on, I kept any of it from affecting me and my performance at work. This was made easier due to the open arms that had welcomed me. My fellow staff members and teachers will never know how much their smiles, greetings, and laughter helped me throughout that point in my life. Along with this, I have enjoyed the connections I have made with so many students. Whether I am joining them for lunch, PE, recess, or reading to them in class, these kids make every day a joy.

I will always remember that day I was given an impromptu interview and will be forever grateful for the chance that was taken on me. Each day as an assistant principal at Webb Elementary, I find more and more that this is most definitely where I need to be. I am so incredibly happy in my new position that I could scream/flip/jump with joy! In fact, I'm pretty certain that I probably could have made this move years ago. I am excited for our future and feel incredibly blessed to be a part of the great things that are happening for our students and the community that surround this school!

***

In *Kids Deserve It!,* I used the analogy of a tree branch and stepping out on it takes risks. When we take that leap of faith, and choose to be brave, yes, sometimes the branch just bends under the weight, and some days it flat-out breaks. What separates the great teachers from the average are those who are willing to step out on a branch even when the one they just stepped on broke right under them.

A STORY FROM BRITTNEY TAYLOR
Nurse Aide

The funny thing about being the nurse aide is that, originally, this was not the job I applied for within the district six years ago. I was going to school to become a teacher, and I was sure that I was going to find a job in the school working in a classroom. In my interview, I was asked how I would handle children who were sick. I can only assume that I answered well because, that same afternoon, I was hired for the nurse aide position! At first, I was so disappointed. I wanted to be a teacher and have those classroom experiences. However, I came to work every day with a smile. I learned the other side to education, which is not teaching but parenting and nurturing. I loved what I did so much that I ended up changing my career path. I received my medical assistant degree, and now I plan to return to school to get my RN license soon! I will never forget the day I realized the kids needed me, and I was created to touch little peoples' lives. Yet the real reward was when I discovered I needed the little people just as much. I could be having one of the hardest days, and some little person would remind me why I am here and how much he or she needs me. At the end of the day, everyone needs to be needed. This is why I love my job.

I truly believe that, deep down, you know if you're where you're supposed to be. I can't tell you how many times people ask me "What's next for you, Todd?" or "Are you leaving Webb this year?" and I always come back to the same thought—being a principal at Webb Elementary in Navasota, Texas, isn't easy. There are many days filled with tears, with doubts, and with me questioning whether I'm the most qualified person for this position. But there are even more days filled with laughter, smiles, and reassurances. Those are the days when . . .

- I get a hug from that child who hasn't been able to stay in class for a full day in over a week because of his anger.
- I cry with a teacher when we are heartbroken to learn that

one of our most "challenging" students is moving away.

- A teacher and I visit a child's home with no other plan than to deliver much-needed groceries.
- My team comes together to pray over a staff member who just lost a loved one.
- I ask for volunteers to stay late to help with a big plan and more than twenty people raise their hands.

It's in the countless moments like those that I know I'm exactly where I'm meant to be. If you're not being challenged, if you're not pushing yourself, and if you're not surrounded by others who will walk alongside you, then you're not where YOU are meant to be.

Being a principal is the hardest job I've ever had—one I could never have imagined myself being in just a few years ago. But this job has fulfilled me like no other job before. And each day on my drive into work, I think about where I'm headed, and I know that Webb Elementary is exactly where I'm meant to be.

THINGS TO CONSIDER

- When did you realize education was where you were meant to be?
- What affirmations have been your little reminders that right here, where you are now, is where you're making an impact?

Tweet your answers and tell your story at #KidsDeserveIt

CHAPTER 35

DEAR ME

So much love and passion went into collecting these stories and creating this book. Writing a book is scary! Never in a million years would I have ever believed I would have not one but two books published.

I've always loved writing, but it took quite a while for me to feel brave enough to share my writing with the world. After the time and effort of writing *Kids Deserve It!* with Adam, I wasn't sure I was ever going to have enough to write another book.

When the idea of *Stories from Webb* came to me, I was sitting with a few of my teachers and listening to them share their brilliance. I'm not saying John C. Webb Elementary in Navasota, Texas, is better than any other school out there. We're not. We still have many kinks we're working out, but we're learning and growing every day. But I thought it would be incredibly cool for the rest of the world to hear from all kinds of people who work on this campus. I wanted to collect examples of their genius and share with the world—with *you*.

As I read and re-read this book, I'm reminded that we all have a story—and that each of us brings something unique and special and wonderful to the table. But there's magic that happens when we decide to be brave and share our stories with others. And you know what? It did take bravery for some of these stories to be told. For some of the educators at Webb Elementary, it was daunting to find their voices and put their stories on paper, knowing others would read them.

My encouragement to you is this: Share your magic. Tell your story. Give a piece of your brilliance to others.

Educating young minds isn't easy, but it changes lives and creates futures. Together we can do this. Together we can change the world, and our #KidsDeserveIt.

To end this book, I have turned to one of my all-time favorite singer-songwriters, Nichole Nordeman, whose beautiful lyrics I have loved since high school. In 2017 she released her first full album of new material in more than a decade. One song in particular I found powerful. It was a song called "Dear Me," written to Nordeman's younger self. It inspired me to do something similar. Here goes …

Dear me,

This is a letter to the boy I used to know.

It's funny how as you grow older and experience different things in life, you begin to see how misguided you were in your youth. Now this letter isn't meant to embarrass you or make you feel like others are judging you.

I want you to know the choices you make as you grow older help you grow into a successful man with a beautiful wife and loving family and friends.

When you're younger, you think everything will be easier as you get older. Life will begin to make more sense. Family will come together. But you need to know that things don't always turn into what you think is right, and that's okay.

Your belief that "if you live in America, you need to know how to speak English" will change. You will learn there's power behind your words and value in learning and growing from others who don't share your beliefs.

You will learn that thinking "welfare is pointless" and "homeless people just need to get a job" are beliefs that are a reflection of you not experiencing as much heartache and trials as others have. You will see the beauty that lies in those broken faces and the changes that come when you bend down to extend a hand instead of rolling your eyes as you walk away.

You will see that love isn't perfect. That image you had in your head of the perfect family isn't a reality. Family is tough. Love is work. But it's work that's worth it. You'll see just how powerful the bonds of family and love can be as you experience the loss of family members and as you take in some of your family when their world falls apart. You'll learn that love means not walking away. You'll learn that love says, "Today isn't easy, it isn't fun, but you mean more to me than taking what I perceive to be the easy road."

You will find you can't change the life of every child you come in contact with. And it will break you the first few times you experience it. But you know what? You never stop trying. Never. Because you will find, many years down the road, that the first child you thought you couldn't help will email you and tell you that you're the only reason they're going to college. And it will fill your heart in ways you've felt few times before. But every child, and every adult, is worth loving in spite of their shortcomings.

You will come to understand that forgiveness isn't easy when others hurt you. But forgiveness is what frees you. It's what makes things better. You often create expectations for friends, family, and colleagues that are unintentionally high. You have to be okay when they don't rise to them. That doesn't mean you lower your expectations, but it does mean you understand that everyone works differently.

Most of all, remember to love freely. With no limits and no expectations. To judge no one. That everyone, regardless of religion, decisions they make in their life, skin color, sexuality, and every choice in between is worthy of your love. Stand up for the quiet. Stand tall in defense of injustice, even when those closest to you sit in silence. Speak love always. Show every living and breathing person that Jesus comes for all of us.

Todd, these aren't lessons you will learn quickly. So don't be afraid to ask questions and know that sometimes it's okay to doubt. But one thing you must never doubt is the love that Jesus has for you.

Love wildly,

Todd

ACKNOWLEDGMENTS

Where do I even begin?

I want to start with my school family at Webb in Navasota ISD. Who knew, when I came to Navasota a few years ago, that we'd be writing a book together? When I had this crazy idea to write with my team, I had no idea it would turn into something so special. There have been many late nights, early mornings, difficult days, and exciting moments, and you guys show up every day ready to tackle it all again. This book is a celebration not only of educators and the great work they do but also of *you*! Thank you for being brave enough to share your stories.

I also want to extend my heartfelt gratitude to the students and families of Webb. We exist as a school for you. We love you guys down to our core.

I have to thank Aaron Marvel, my right hand when starting out in Navasota. For over three years, we laughed together, cried together, gave each other a hard time, played pranks, and kept each other humble and somewhat sane. Aaron, I know our school is what it is today because you were here. I am the principal I am today, in part, because of you. You helped keep me calm, and you were never afraid to speak your mind. Even though you've moved to another state and are pursuing your passion, you will always play a vital role in what Webb Elementary is—and who I am—today!

I can't go without also thanking Kim Bearden. Kim has been an educational hero of mine for years. The fact that I can now also call her my friend blows my mind. Kim, thank you for always being such an encourager to not only me but also to so many others in our field. You have supported me, built me up, challenged me, and most of all, been there every time I've needed you. Even when you've had a thousand things on your plate, you've always come through, and you are a part of the Webb Elementary story. One that will never be forgotten. There are few people in the world I admire and respect as much as you, and I don't think you'll ever understand the impact you've had on this school and me.

To my friends and family. Those who listen to me vent, allow me to cry on their shoulders, remind me of who I truly am, those who tell me to chill out, and the ones who answer my rambling phone calls or Voxer messages, you know who you are. Thank you for showing me what it feels like to have a support system that keeps you humble and walks alongside you.

Dave and Shelley Burgess. Where do I even begin? Not only did you take a risk by believing in the mission of *Kids Deserve It!*, but you also decided to take this leap again with me. You let me express my thoughts, emotions, and always allowed me to be as creative as I wished. You are great friends and even better mentors. Thank you for helping me find my voice.

To my wife Liz. You've dealt with the crazy hours, countless trips, days spent writing and working. We've gotten to travel the world together and spend many days at home just enjoying the peace and quiet. You are my better half, and God really decided to spoil me when he brought you into my life. Thank you for always letting me follow my dreams.

And finally to you. Yes, you. The person reading this book right now. It's wild to me that people around the world care to read the words I've placed on these pages. Thank you for all that you bring to this world. Thank you for wanting to better yourself. Thank you for loving kids. Thank you for supporting this book and it's message. I hope that you choose to be brave, love wildly, take risks, embrace the challenges, and most of all, remember that every moment is an opportunity to be better. It's a scary thing, but just like my team and I did in this book, we need you to share your story! Write a blog, tweet it out, share it on Facebook, but get out there and share your brilliance with the world. We need your stories too.

DAVE BURGESS Consulting, Inc.

TEACH LIKE A PIRATE
Increase Student Engagement, Boost Your Creativity,
and Transform Your Life as an Educator
By Dave Burgess (@BurgessDave)

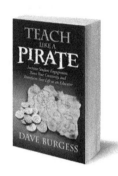

Teach Like a PIRATE is the New York Times' best-selling book that has sparked a worldwide educational revolution. It is part inspirational manifesto that ignites passion for the profession and part practical road map filled with dynamic strategies to dramatically increase student engagement. Translated into multiple languages, its message resonates with educators who want to design outrageously creative lessons and transform school into a life-changing experience for students.

P IS FOR PIRATE
Inspirational ABC's for Educators
By Dave and Shelley Burgess (@Burgess_Shelley)

Teaching is an adventure that stretches the imagination and calls for creativity every day! In *P is for Pirate*, husband and wife team, Dave and Shelley Burgess, encourage and inspire educators to make their classrooms fun and exciting places to learn. Tapping into years of personal experience and drawing on the insights of more than seventy educators, the authors offer a wealth of ideas for making learning and teaching more fulfilling than ever before.

THE INNOVATOR'S MINDSET
Empower Learning, Unleash Talent, and Lead a Culture of Creativity
By George Couros (@gcouros)

The traditional system of education requires students to hold their questions and compliantly stick to the scheduled curriculum. But our job as educators is to provide new and better opportunities for our students. It's time to recognize that compliance doesn't foster innovation, encourage critical thinking, or inspire creativity—and those are the skills our students need to succeed. In *The Innovator's Mindset*, George Couros encourages teachers and administrators to empower their learners to wonder, to explore—and to become forward-thinking leaders.

PURE GENIUS
Building a Culture of Innovation and Taking 20% Time to the Next Level
By Don Wettrick (@DonWettrick)

For far too long, schools have been bastions of boredom, killers of creativity, and way too comfortable with compliance and conformity. In *Pure Genius*, Don Wettrick explains how collaboration—with experts, students, and other educators—can help you create interesting, and even life-changing, opportunities for learning. Wettrick's book inspires and equips educators with a systematic blueprint for teaching innovation in any school.

LEARN LIKE A PIRATE
Empower Your Students to Collaborate, Lead, and Succeed

By Paul Solarz (@PaulSolarz)

Today's job market demands that students be prepared to take responsibility for their lives and careers. We do them a disservice if we teach them how to earn passing grades without equipping them to take charge of their education. In *Learn Like a PIRATE*, Paul Solarz explains how to design classroom experiences that encourage students to take risks and explore their passions in a stimulating, motivating, and supportive environment where improvement, rather than grades, is the focus. Discover how student-led classrooms help students thrive and develop into self-directed, confident citizens who are capable of making smart, responsible decisions, all on their own.

DITCH THAT TEXTBOOK
Free Your Teaching and Revolutionize Your Classroom

By Matt Miller (@jmattmiller)

Textbooks are symbols of centuries-old education. They're often outdated as soon as they hit students' desks. Acting "by the textbook" implies compliance and a lack of creativity. It's time to ditch those textbooks—and those textbook assumptions about learning! In *Ditch That Textbook*, teacher and blogger Matt Miller encourages educators to throw out meaningless, pedestrian teaching and learning practices. He empowers them to evolve and improve on old, standard, teaching methods. Ditch That Textbook is a support system, toolbox, and manifesto to help educators free their teaching and revolutionize their classrooms.

50 THINGS YOU CAN DO WITH GOOGLE CLASSROOM
By Alice Keeler and Libbi Miller (@alicekeeler, @MillerLibbi)

It can be challenging to add new technology to the classroom, but it's a must if students are going to be well-equipped for the future. Alice Keeler and Libbi Miller shorten the learning curve by providing a thorough overview of the Google Classroom App. Part of Google Apps for Education (GAfE), Google Classroom was specifically designed to help teachers save time by streamlining the process of going digital. Complete with screenshots, *50 Things You Can Do with Google Classroom* provides ideas and step-by-step instructions to help teachers implement this powerful tool.

50 THINGS TO GO FURTHER WITH GOOGLE CLASSROOM
A Student-Centered Approach

By Alice Keeler and Libbi Miller (@alicekeeler, @MillerLibbi)

Today's technology empowers educators to move away from the traditional classroom where teachers lead and students work independently—each doing the same thing. In *50 Things to Go Further with Google Classroom: A Student-Centered Approach*, authors and educators Alice Keeler and Libbi Miller offer inspiration and resources to help you create a digitally rich, engaging, student-centered environment. They show you how to tap into the power of individualized learning that is possible with Google Classroom.

140 TWITTER TIPS FOR EDUCATORS
Get Connected, Grow Your Professional Learning Network, and Reinvigorate Your Career
By Brad Currie, Billy Krakower, and Scott Rocco (@bradmcurrie, @wkrakower, @ScottRRocco)

Whatever questions you have about education or about how you can be even better at your job, you'll find ideas, resources, and a vibrant network of professionals ready to help you on Twitter. In *140 Twitter Tips for Educators*, #Satchat hosts and founders of Evolving Educators, Brad Currie, Billy Krakower, and Scott Rocco, offer step-by-step instructions to help you master the basics of Twitter, build an online following, and become a Twitter rock star.

MASTER THE MEDIA
How Teaching Media Literacy Can Save Our Plugged-in World
By Julie Smith (@julnilsmith)

Written to help teachers and parents educate the next generation, *Master the Media* explains the history, purpose, and messages behind the media. The point isn't to get kids to unplug; it's to help them make informed choices, understand the difference between truth and lies, and discern perception from reality. Critical thinking leads to smarter decisions—and it's why media literacy can save the world.

THE ZEN TEACHER
Creating Focus, Simplicity, and Tranquility in the Classroom
By Dan Tricarico (@thezenteacher)

Teachers have incredible power to influence—even improve—the future. In *The Zen Teacher*, educator, blogger, and speaker Dan Tricarico provides practical, easy-to-use techniques to help teachers be their best—unrushed and fully focused—so they can maximize their performance and improve their quality of life. In this introductory guide, Dan Tricarico explains what it means to develop a Zen practice—something that has nothing to do with religion and everything to do with your ability to thrive in the classroom.

EXPLORE LIKE A PIRATE
Gamification and Game-Inspired Course Design to Engage, Enrich, and Elevate Your Learners
By Michael Matera (@MrMatera)

Are you ready to transform your classroom into an experiential world that flourishes on collaboration and creativity? Then set sail with classroom game designer and educator Michael Matera as he reveals the possibilities and power of game-based learning. In *eXPlore Like a Pirate*, Matera serves as your experienced guide to help you apply the most motivational techniques of gameplay to your classroom. You'll learn gamification strategies that will work with and enhance (rather than replace) your current curriculum and discover how these engaging methods can be applied to any grade level or subject.

YOUR SCHOOL ROCKS ... SO TELL PEOPLE!
Passionately Pitch and Promote the Positives Happening on Your Campus

By Ryan McLane and Eric Lowe (@McLane_Ryan, @EricLowe21)

Great things are happening in your school every day. The problem is, no one beyond your school walls knows about them. School principals Ryan McLane and Eric Lowe want to help you get the word out! In *Your School Rocks ... So Tell People!* McLane and Lowe offer more than seventy immediately actionable tips along with easy-to-follow instructions and links to video tutorials. This practical guide will equip you to create an effective and manageable communication strategy using social media tools. Learn how to keep your students' families and community connected, informed, and excited about what's going on in your school.

PLAY LIKE A PIRATE
Engage Students with Toys, Games, and Comics
By Quinn Rollins (@jedikermit)

Yes! Serious learning can be seriously fun. In *Play Like a Pirate*, Quinn Rollins offers practical, engaging strategies and resources that make it easy to integrate fun into your curriculum. Regardless of the grade level you teach, you'll find inspiration and ideas that will help you engage your students in unforgettable ways.

THE CLASSROOM CHEF
Sharpen your lessons. Season your classes. Make math meaningful.
By John Stevens and Matt Vaudrey (@Jstevens009, @MrVaudrey)

In *The Classroom Chef*, math teachers and instructional coaches John Stevens and Matt Vaudrey share their secret recipes, ingredients, and tips for serving up lessons that engage students and help them "get" math. You can use these ideas and methods as-is, or better yet, tweak them and create your own enticing educational meals. The message the authors share is that, with imagination and preparation, every teacher can be a Classroom Chef.

HOW MUCH WATER DO WE HAVE?
5 Success Principles for Conquering Any Challenge and Thriving in Times of Change
By Pete Nunweiler with Kris Nunweiler

In *How Much Water Do We Have?* Pete Nunweiler identifies five key elements—information, planning, motivation, support, and leadership—that are necessary for the success of any goal, life transition, or challenge. Referring to these elements as the 5 Waters of Success, Pete explains that like the water we drink, you need them to thrive in today's rapidly paced world. If you're feeling stressed out, overwhelmed, or uncertain at work or at home, pause and look for the signs of dehydration. Learn how to find, acquire, and use the 5 Waters of Success—so you can share them with your team and family members.

THE WRITING ON THE CLASSROOM WALL
How Posting Your Most Passionate Beliefs about Education Can Empower Your Students, Propel Your Growth, and Lead to a Lifetime of Learning

By Steve Wyborney (@SteveWyborney)

In *The Writing on the Classroom Wall*, Steve Wyborney explains how posting and discussing Big Ideas can lead to deeper learning. You'll learn why sharing your ideas will sharpen and refine them. You'll also be encouraged to know that the Big Ideas you share don't have to be profound to make a profound impact on learning. In fact, Steve explains, it's okay if some of your ideas fall off the wall. What matters most is sharing them.

KIDS DESERVE IT!
Pushing Boundaries and Challenging Conventional Thinking
By Todd Nesloney and Adam Welcome (@TechNinjaTodd, @awelcome)

In *Kids Deserve It!*, Todd and Adam encourage you to think big and make learning fun and meaningful for students. Their high-tech, high-touch, and highly engaging practices will inspire you to take risks, shake up the status quo, and be a champion for your students. While you're at it, you just might rediscover why you became an educator in the first place.

LAUNCH
Using Design Thinking to Boost Creativity and Bring Out the Maker in Every Student
By John Spencer and A.J. Juliani (@spencerideas, @ajjuliani)

Something happens in students when they define themselves as makers and inventors and creators. They discover powerful skills—problem-solving, critical thinking, and imagination—that will help them shape the world's future … our future. In *LAUNCH*, John Spencer and A.J. Juliani provide a process that can be incorporated into every class at every grade level … even if you don't consider yourself a "creative teacher." And if you dare to innovate and view creativity as an essential skill, you will empower your students to change the world—starting right now.

INSTANT RELEVANCE
Using Today's Experiences to Teach Tomorrow's Lessons
By Denis Sheeran (@MathDenisNJ)

Every day students in schools around the world ask the question, "When am I ever going to use this in real life?" In *Instant Relevance*, author and keynote speaker Denis Sheeran equips you to create engaging lessons from experiences and events that matter to your students. Learn how to help your students see meaningful connections between the real world and what they learn in the classroom—because that's when learning sticks.

ESCAPING THE SCHOOL LEADER'S DUNK TANK
How to Prevail When Others Want to See You Drown
By Rebecca Coda and Rick Jetter (@RebeccaCoda, @RickJetter)

No school leader is immune to the effects of discrimination, bad politics, revenge, or ego-driven coworkers. These kinds of dunk-tank situations can make an educator's life miserable. By sharing real-life stories and insightful research, the authors (who are dunk-tank survivors themselves) equip school leaders with the practical knowledge and emotional tools necessary to survive and, better yet, avoid getting "dunked."

START. RIGHT. NOW.
Teach and Lead for Excellence
By Todd Whitaker, Jeff Zoul, and Jimmy Casas (@ToddWhitaker, @Jeff_Zoul, @casas_jimmy)

In their work leading up to *Start. Right. Now.* Todd Whitaker, Jeff Zoul, and Jimmy Casas studied educators from across the nation and discovered four key behaviors of excellence: Excellent leaders and teachers Know the Way, Show the Way, Go the Way, and Grow Each Day. If you are ready to take the first step toward excellence, this motivating book will put you on the right path.

LEAD LIKE A PIRATE
Make School Amazing for Your Students and Staff
By Shelley Burgess and Beth Houf (@Burgess_Shelley, @BethHouf)

In *Lead Like a PIRATE*, education leaders Shelley Burgess and Beth Houf map out the character traits necessary to captain a school or district. You'll learn where to find the treasure that's already in your classrooms and schools—and how to bring out the very best in your educators. This book will equip and encourage you to be relentless in your quest to make school amazing for your students, staff, parents, and communities.

TEACHING MATH WITH GOOGLE APPS
50 G Suite Activities
By Alice Keeler and Diana Herrington (@AliceKeeler, @mathdiana)

Google Apps give teachers the opportunity to interact with students in a more meaningful way than ever before, while G Suite empowers students to be creative, critical thinkers who collaborate as they explore and learn. In *Teaching Math with Google Apps*, educators Alice Keeler and Diana Herrington demonstrate fifty different ways to bring math classes into the twenty-first century with easy-to-use technology.

TABLE TALK MATH
A Practical Guide for Bringing Math into Everyday Conversations
By John Stevens (@Jstevens009)

Making math part of families' everyday conversations is a powerful way to help children and teens learn to love math. In *Table Talk Math*, John Stevens offers parents (and teachers!) ideas for initiating authentic, math-based conversations that will get kids to notice and be curious about all the numbers, patterns, and equations in the world around them.

SHIFT THIS!
How to Implement Gradual Change for Massive Impact in Your Classroom
By Joy Kirr (@JoyKirr)

Establishing a student-led culture that isn't focused on grades and homework but on individual responsibility and personalized learning may seem like a daunting task—especially if you think you have to do it all at once. But significant change is possible, sustainable, and even easy when it happens little by little. In *Shift This!* educator and speaker Joy Kirr explains how to make gradual shifts—in your thinking, teaching, and approach to classroom design—that will have a massive impact in your classroom. Make the first shift today!

UNMAPPED POTENTIAL
An Educator's Guide to Lasting Change
By Julie Hasson and Missy Lennard (@PPrincipals)

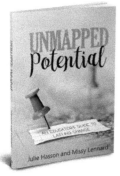

No matter where you are in your educational career, chances are you have, at times, felt overwhelmed and overworked. Maybe you feel that way right now. If so, you aren't alone. But the more important news is that things can get better! You simply need the right map to guide you from frustrated to fulfilled. *Unmapped Potential* offers advice and practical strategies to help you find your unique path to becoming the kind of educator—the kind of person—you want to be.

SHATTERING THE PERFECT TEACHER MYTH
6 Truths That Will Help You THRIVE as an Educator
By Aaron Hogan (@aaron_hogan)

The idyllic myth of the perfect teacher perpetuates unrealistic expectations that erode self-confidence and set teachers up for failure. Author and educator Aaron Hogan is on a mission to shatter the myth of the perfect teacher by equipping educators with strategies that help them shift out of survival mode and THRIVE.

SOCIAL LEADIA
Moving Students from Digital Citizenship to Digital Leadership
By Jennifer Casa-Todd (@JCasaTodd)

Equipping students for their future begins by helping them become digital leaders now. In our networked society, students need to learn how to leverage social media to connect to people, passions, and opportunities to grow and make a difference. *Social LEADia* offers insight and engaging stories to help you shift the focus at school and at home from digital citizenship to digital leadership.

SPARK LEARNING
3 Keys to Embracing the Power of Student Curiosity
By Ramsey Musallam (@ramusallam)

Inspired by his popular TED Talk "*3 Rules to Spark Learning*," this book combines brain science research, proven teaching methods, and Ramsey's personal story to empower you to improve your students' learning experiences by inspiring inquiry and harnessing its benefits. If you want to engage students in more interesting and effective learning, this is the book for you.

DITCH THAT HOMEWORK
Practical Strategies to Help Make Homework Obsolete
By Matt Miller and Alice Keeler (@jmattmiller, @alicekeeler)

In *Ditch That Homework*, Matt Miller and Alice Keeler discuss the pros and cons of homework, why teachers assign it, and what life could look like without it. As they evaluate the research and share parent and teacher insights, the authors offer a convincing case for ditching homework and replacing it with more effective and personalized learning methods.

THE FOUR O'CLOCK FACULTY
A Rogue Guide to Revolutionizing Professional Development
By Rich Czyz (@RACzyz)

Author Rich Czyz is on a mission to revolutionize professional learning for all educators. In *The Four O'Clock Faculty*, Rich identifies ways to make PD meaningful, efficient, and, above all, personally relevant. This book is a practical guide that reveals why some professional development (PD) is so awful and what you can do to change the model for the betterment of you and your colleagues.

CULTURIZE
Every Student. Every Day. Whatever It Takes.
By Jimmy Casas (@casas_jimmy)

In *Culturize*, author and education leader Jimmy Casas shares insights into what it takes to cultivate a community of learners who embody the innately human traits our world desperately needs, such as kindness, honesty, and compassion. His stories reveal how these "soft skills" can be honed while meeting and exceeding academic standards of twenty-first-century learning.

CODE BREAKER
Increase Creativity, Remix Assessment, and Develop a Class of Coder Ninjas!
By Brian Aspinall (@mraspinall)

Code Breaker equips you to use coding in your classroom to turn curriculum expectations into skills. Students learn how to identify problems, develop solutions, and use computational thinking to apply and demonstrate their learning. Best of all, you don't have to be a "computer geek" to empower your students with these essential skills.

THE WILD CARD
7 Steps to an Educator's Creative Breakthrough
By Hope and Wade King (@hopekingteach, @wadeking7)

Have you ever wished you were more creative . . . or that your students were more engaged in your lessons? *The Wild Card* is your step-by-step guide to experiencing a creative breakthrough in your classroom with your students. Wade and Hope King show you how to draw on your authentic self to deliver your content creatively and be the wild card who changes the game for your learners.

ABOUT THE AUTHOR

Todd Nesloney is an educator down to his core. Whether it's working with kids or adults, Todd loves sharing his passion of learning. He currently serves as the principal and lead learner at Webb Elementary in Navasota, Texas. Prior to working in this capacity, Todd served for a year as principal at Navasota Intermediate and has taught in the fourth and fifth grades for seven years at Fields Store Elementary in Waller, Texas.

Todd was recognized by President Barack Obama as a White House Champion of Change and by the National School Board Association as a "20 to Watch" in Education. He was recognized by the Texas Computer Education Association (TCEA) as their Elementary Teacher of the Year and selected by the Center for Digital Education as one of the "Top 40 Innovators in Education." He was the 2015 BAMMY Award recipient for Elementary Principal of the Year and the 2014 BAMMY Award recipient for Classroom Teacher of the Year.

Todd is the author of children's book, *Spruce & Lucy*, and co-author of the award-winning book *Flipping 2.0: Practical Strategies for Flipping Your Classroom*, as well as the co-author of *Kids Deserve It!* Todd also co-hosts a top-rated iTunes show, *Kids Deserve It!*

Todd is passionate about eliminating excuses, innovative practices, and doing what's best for kids. In addition to his career as an administrator and educator, Todd leads staff developments and gives keynotes at districts and conferences around the world.

In his time off, Todd loves to go to the movies, read, garden, and spend his time with his wife, Lissette.

You can learn more about Todd by visiting his website: toddnesloney.com.

Connect with him on Twitter: @TechNinjaTodd.

CPSIA information can be obtained
at www.ICGtesting.com
Printed in the USA
LVHW01s1018220118
563286LV00007B/9/P